SPORTS
IN
LINCOLN COUNTY

One band that graced the gridiron of the old Lincolnton High School Love Field stands in formation for this photograph by Clyde "Baby Ray" Cornwell during the early 1940s. S. Ray Lowder started the first band at Lincolnton High during the early 1930s. The old Love Field is currently the parking lot of Lincoln Campus of Gaston College. Though the field is gone, many Lincolntonians have fond memories of playing there and listening to the cheers from roaring crowds. (Lincoln County Museum of History.)

FRONT COVER: Dennis Byrd (front cover inset) stands ready in his Lincolnton High football uniform during the time he served as a lineman. Under coaches Von Ray Harris, Don Pack, and Roy Turbyfill, Byrd received All–Southwestern Conference honors three years in a row. As Lincolnton's first All-American football player, the city held a "Dennis Byrd Night" and presented him the key to the city and other mementos. In addition to his accolades as a football player, he was also on the basketball team. In four years as center, Byrd scored over 1,000 points. (Courtesy of Paul and Jennifer Byrd.)
COVER BACKGROUND: The background image is the 1931 Lincolnton High School Basketball team. Photographers used the school as a background for many team photographs over the years. (LCMH.)
BACK COVER: Shown on the back cover is the "Dedication of Lights" at North Lincoln High School's baseball stadium in 2006. (Courtesy Patty Skidmore.)

SPORTS IN LINCOLN COUNTY

Jason L. Harpe

ARCADIA PUBLISHING

ISBN 978-0-7385-4401-4

Published by Arcadia Publishing
Charleston SC, Chicago IL, Portsmouth NH, San Francisco CA

Printed in the United States of America

Library of Congress Catalog Card Number: 2006935612

For all general information contact Arcadia Publishing at:
Telephone 843-853-2070
Fax 843-853-0044
E-mail sales@arcadiapublishing.com
For customer service and orders:
Toll-Free 1-888-313-2665

Visit us on the Internet at www.arcadiapublishing.com

This photograph served as an appropriate introduction to the athletics section of Lincolnton High's 1961 yearbook. It was during this season that the football team won the Southwestern AAA conference championship. Bobby Beal used this image to commemorate his athletic career at Lincolnton High School in a personalized scrapbook that he maintains today. (Courtesy of Bobby Beal.)

CONTENTS

ACKNOWLEDGMENTS

For this project, the citizens of Lincoln County welcomed me into their homes to reminisce over sports photographs and memories. Many people approved of and assisted my attempts to commemorate the history of sports in Lincoln County through photographs. Not only did these people provide access to their collections, but they also put me in contact with others who maintained collections of the same size or larger.

We are lucky to have the Lincoln County Sports Hall of Fame, composed of a dedicated group of former athletes that work incessantly to honor men and women who made indelible marks in the sports community over the past 100 years. They have inducted some great athletes, trainers, and enthusiasts over the past six years and have another great slate of inductees for 2006. Without the efforts of their board of directors and others, this book would have never come to fruition. I extend special thanks to them for allowing me space on various agendas to discuss this project.

I owe a debt of gratitude to Roby Jetton for the countless hours he has spent on the phone with me reviewing lists of athletes and teams from across the county to be included in this book. With him, I conducted a few interesting interviews with athletes such as Pete Crow that contributed important information on athletics in Lincoln County.

Thanks to the following lenders for so graciously opening their scrapbooks and files to me: Mary Long Abernathy, Hilmi Ari, Steve Bailey, Henry Barkley, Bobby Beal, Wes Beam, Lee Boyd, Polly Bryant, Paul and Jennifer Byrd, Kevin Cherry, Kelly Childers, Alice Clanton, Mike and Libby Cline, Micah Cline, Scott Cloninger, Ralph Connor, Debbie Cornwell, Leslie Costner, Pete Crow, Jack Dellinger, Darrell Harkey, Paul Haynes, Steve Herman, Roby Jetton, Lincoln County Sports Hall of Fame, Barry Long, Andy Mauney, Ken McCurry, Lynne Millwood, John Henry Moss, David Napier, Betty G. Ross, Sally Rudisill, Patty Skidmore, Richard Smith, and Bobby Turner.

Thanks to Nancy Anthony for her search for local newspaper articles on sports in Lincoln County from the early 20th century to the present. Thanks to Matt Boles for his continued interest in Lincoln County history and his help finding photographs from eastern Lincoln County.

INTRODUCTION

Lincoln County has a long and reputable history and heritage that includes judges, generals, historians, textile entrepreneurs, iron manufacturers, educators, and other professionals who have contributed to the economic, political, and educational development of Lincoln County and North Carolina. These individuals occupy prominent places in the documented records of Lincoln County's past. From the records, chroniclers and historians have pulled biographical information to spotlight these individuals' successes and contributions to the growth and reputation of Lincoln County. Prominent men and women held the means and influence to build Lincoln County's most imposing homes, serve as stockholders in Lincolnton's early banks, make major decisions regarding the county's services and resources, and affect change in the social and cultural history of the county.

Sports and athletics are hard to find in any of Lincoln County's recorded or published histories, with the exception of a few publications produced by the Lincoln County Historical Association. Though this has been neglected for many years, Lincoln County newspapers are full of articles, photographs, and advertisements about baseball, football, basketball, boxing, and other athletic activities taking place on ball fields, in gymnasiums, and at parks in the county. From the earliest reports during the first decade of the 20th century about a Lincolnton baseball team playing against colleges and a group of Native Americans from Cherokee, North Carolina, to recent local reporters whose sole responsibility is to document sports in the county, athletics has occupied an important place in the social history of the county.

Local teams and ballparks afforded county folks an opportunity to invest time in a recreational endeavor that built pride in their local community and the men and women that worked incessantly to entertain the crowds. From as early as the first decade of the 20th century, men such as Edgar Love—cotton manufacturer, mayor of Lincolnton, and sports enthusiast—spent money to assemble a team that could defeat the Charlotte Hornets and other established teams from the Piedmont of North Carolina. These teams were the predecessors of clubs at Lincolnton High School and other county teams that reaped the benefits of instruction from leaders such as C. D. "Block" Smith, Willie Hull, Lyle Edwards, Elizabeth Hoke, F. D. "Jack" Kiser, and many other coaches from the 1960s to the present.

What these coaches and players brought to the citizens of Lincolnton and Lincoln County was an entertaining and competitive outlet that transported them from the mundane, uneventful, and lackluster days spent in the mills, fields, and behind desks throughout the county. Whether at a football game at Lincolnton High's Love Field, a baseball or softball game near Boger and Crawford Mills during an annual field day, or a Friday night under the lights at one of Lincoln County's football stadiums, athletics touches some aspects of each person in Lincoln County. Whether as a participant or a spectator, the smell of freshly cut grass, pine tar, tobacco, sweat, and victory pervades the lives of the young and old throughout the county. Men and women remember how it felt to be at the game at Love Field in May 1940, when the Boger and Crawford Mills baseball team beat a team from Rock Hill, South Carolina, at the first game under lights in county history. Others remember the feeling after seeing or hearing of the state championships won by East Lincoln High School's girls' basketball team during the 1972–1973 season, the Lincolnton High School football state championship in 1993, the Lincolnton High School baseball state championship in 1995, or the West Lincoln High School wrestling state championship in 2000.

This small volume serves only to introduce an important subject matter through photographs to the citizens of Lincoln County, both young and old. It is not meant to be an all-inclusive volume that spotlights each individual and team that made an indelible mark on the fabric of sports in Lincoln County. My hope is that people (athletes, spectators, and supporters) will take the time to reminisce over the periods they spent on the ball field or in the gym playing, coaching, or cheering and realize how important each coach and fellow athlete has been. I will never forget a comment made to me by one of my coaches, who said that we should "enjoy every single minute, with every person, because this is the best time of your life; before you know it, you will be off the field and away from the best experience that life provides."

The purpose of *Sports in Lincoln County* is to help transport you back to the best time of your life and to inspire you to give back to the next generation of athletes that are coming of age right before you.

I dedicate this volume to the many baseball, basketball, and football coaches that never let me settle for mediocre performances and to my father and mother, who gave everything they had to make me a better athlete and student.

1

BASEBALL

America's favorite pastime reached Lincoln County during the first decade of the 20th century. The first organized teams wore unofficial uniforms, played teams from all over North Carolina, and traveled in cars that traversed county roads with lights provided by kerosene lamps. Lincolnton's earliest team included players who had experience participating in other leagues and in college. During the 1920s and 1930s, various mill owners organized teams and recruited players from surrounding counties to build their rosters and enhance the teams' talent. Investing in wool and cotton uniforms with the names of their mills emblazoned upon their players' chests, these mills owners took pride in their teams' inclusion in organized leagues. As crowds assembled in the stadium at Love Field and other sites across the Piedmont, men played from the heart and reveled in the love of the game.

As leagues such as the Western Carolina, Sally, and Mid-State began to form throughout North Carolina, owners of teams in Lincolnton joined these leagues and brought the excitement and competition to the people of the county. Teams such as the Lincolnton Red Sox and Lincolnton Cardinals employed charismatic and productive players that brought notoriety and success to the county. These teams not only featured players that went on to play with other semi-professional and professional teams, but also trained players that stayed in their local community and instilled in young men the appreciation and love of the game. The winning tradition in Lincoln County established by these teams foreshadowed the professional careers of players such as Tony Cloninger, Steve Herman, Richard Smith, and Jay Heafner.

The winning baseball tradition in Lincoln County that early teams built led to many later winning records and a state championship at Lincolnton High School in 1995.

Assembled on the steps of the Lincoln County Courthouse, the earliest photographed group of athletes from Lincoln County poses in various uniforms for this c. 1902 photograph. Team members include, from left to right, (first row) Kemp Battle Nixon, Guy E. Cline, ? Shell, Harris Burgin, and Herbert Yount; (second row) Walter N. Keener, ? Burgin, and John Davenport; (third row) Joseph Nixon, J. L. Lineberger, J. Edgar Love, and Ben Hilderbrand. (LCMH.)

Kemp Battle Nixon poses in his batting stance in 1907 for Trinity College (now Duke University). Nixon attended Lincoln County schools and entered the University of North Carolina in 1901. Upon graduation in 1905, he studied law at Trinity, where he also played football. He received his degree in 1907 and worked for Congressman E. Y. Webb in Washington, D.C. He returned home to open a law office in February 1908. Nixon practiced law for over 40 years, chaired the Lincoln County Board of Education for 14 years, served as a state senator from 1931 to 1935, and was elected recorder court judge in 1936. It has been written that "horses, cattle, football, and baseball" were the judge's main hobbies. (LCMH.)

As one of Lincolnton's first organized baseball teams, these men won a championship in a league that featured teams from North and South Carolina in 1919. Team members are, from left to right, (first row) Edgar Love Jr. (batboy), Larry Beal, Robby Robinson, Charlie Tilson (manager), Charles Beal, Jennings "Chink" Edwards, and John Herndon (sportswriter); (second row) Frank Love, Jim Shuford, Tom Gheen, Bill Hoffman, Whitfield Tobey, Coy Stamey, and Fred "Dad" Broome. (LCMH.)

BASE BALL!

Monday and Tuesday.

Lincolnton

—VS.—

Lenoir

AT HORSESHOE PARK.

Game Called Monday 5 o'clock Tuesday 4 o'clock

Everybody come and root for the Home Team.

Admission, each person, 25 cents.

This c. 1910 flyer promoted a baseball game between Lincolnton and Lenoir College in Hickory. The 25¢ admission for this game at Horseshoe Park in Lincolnton supported the local United Daughters of the Confederacy. Lincolnton defeated Lenoir College 7-5, and Lincolnton's Earl Padgett was compared to Ty Cobb. Other Lincolnton games during the decade featured squads from various areas and a group of Cherokees in 1911. One of the fields on which these teams played in 1911 was located near the waterworks plant alongside the Carolina an Northwestern (C&NW) tracks. (LCMH.)

In the early 20th century, before radio broadcasts brought major-league games into homes, young men organized baseball teams in many small towns, mill villages, and rural communities. In this c. 1918 photograph, the Triangle baseball team is clad in wool uniforms with high stockings and equipped with mitts and bats. From left to right are (first row) Dallas Barker and Marian Proctor; (second row) Harvey Cherry, Joe Cherry, Robert Nixon, and Rozzelle Proctor; (third row) Joe Graham, Etheridge Cherry, and Fred Long. (Courtesy of Mary Long Abernathy.)

Members of the Lincolnton High "L" Club in 1923, include Howell G. Gabriel (president), Loy Heavner (vice president), Kenneth Goodson (secretary-treasurer), Ralph Parker, David Lore, Forest Smith, Lindsey Hunter, George Crowell, Robert Boyd (director), Kenneth Heavner, Clyde Abernathy, Robert Dellinger, Aubrey Shives, Frank Gamble, Rudolph Shives, Kenneth Goodson, Lawrence Warlick, James Putnam, John Senter, Ralph Cochrane, Carl Marlow, Austin Abernathy, and D. C. Leonard. (Courtesy of Betty G. Ross.)

Baseball players from western Lincoln County (either Bess Chapel or North Brook) are, from left to right, (first row) unidentified, Willie Hull, and Ralph Hull; (second row) ? Heavner, unidentified, and Blanch Heavner; (third row) Floyd Beam and unidentified; (fourth row) unidentified, ? Brown, and Ray Beam. Willie Hull (1896–1973) was the son of Robert and Myra Eaker Hull of the North Brook community. He taught in Lincoln County for 45 years, was principal of North Brook No. 3 School for 30 years, a member of the Lincoln County School Board for 8 years, a member of the North Carolina Association of Educators, and a justice of the peace for 20 years. (LCMH.)

Charles D. "Block" Smith, the second player from the left on the second row, was one of the earliest athletes and coaches in Lincoln County. Smith coached every male sports team at Lincolnton High over a period of 12 years (1925–1937); his record in football was 62-40-11, 126-71 in basketball, and a remarkable 140-43 in baseball. Smith departed Lincolnton to coach at Guilford College in Greensboro, and he died in 1944 while in the military in Key West, Florida. In 1954, Lincoln County dedicated a new gymnasium in his name. (LCMH.)

Lincolnton High boys' baseball team members in 1931, include Charles "Block" Smith, coach; D. Wilkenson, manager; J. C. Pruitt and J. Rudisill, assistant managers; L. Elmore, catcher; C. Broome, pitcher; J. Broome, first base; B. Mauney, second base; E. Goodson, third base; E. Rudisill, shortstop; Y. Ward, left field; R. Rudisill, center field; F. Rudisill, right field; J. Rudisill, pitcher; R. Little, sub-catcher; M. Lingerfelt, sub-pitcher; E. Caldwell, sub-first base; R. Yoder, sub-second base; W. Ramsey, sub-third base; B. Goodson, sub-shortstop; G. Digh, sub-left field; R. Mincy, sub-center field; J. C. Burke, sub-right field; and C. Dellinger, sub-pitcher. Also listed are the "Scrubs:" B. Mauney, J. Reinhardt, S. Kale, J. Lee, G. Keener, F. Houser, and P. Kistler. (LCMH.)

Jay Shuford Boggs picked up a baseball and bat for the first time at age six at Cherryville High. He was on the Cherryville team that won the Western North Carolina Championship at Chapel Hill in 1917. He is shown here (at far right) around 1930 as the manager of the Judson Mill baseball team of Greenville, South Carolina, with baseball legend Connie Mack, who won five World Series and 3,776 wins as a manager. After his baseball career, Boggs resided in Lincoln County. (Courtesy of Polly Boggs Bryant.)

The Boger and Crawford Mills baseball players, pictured around 1930, are, from left to right, (first row) Jimmie Clanton (child), Ernest Featherstone, Adrain Clanton, Everette Dellinger, Peg Proctor, and Red Holbrooks; (second row) Red Dellinger, Jud McGinnis, Smack Proctor, Buck Goodson, Buck Mauney, and Sid Reep; (third row) Marshall Beal, unidentified, William Bumgarner, Guy Cline Sr., and Burl Long; (fourth row) Clyde Lawing, John Dellinger, Bill Goodson, Carl Dysert, and Rob Rudisill. (Courtesy of Alice Clanton.)

Boger and Crawford Mills baseball players pictured here in the 1930s are featured throughout the book. Many participated in other teams statewide in the Sally League, Western Carolina League, and Mid-State League. Robert Boger, a Philadelphia native, built the Boger and Crawford Mill in 1919 in an area that was once called Goodsonville. Over almost 25 years, Boger built a successful baseball team that included players who went on to play in other leagues. (Courtesy of Barry Long.)

The 1940 Boger and Crawford Mills baseball team won a tri-county league pennant with a record of 43-9. Members include, from left to right, (first row) Jim Warren (scorekeeper), Kelly Kee, Chunk Rudisill, Dopey Frye, Pete Crow, and Peg Proctor (batboy); (second row) Rob Rudisill, Bain Sisk, Bob Beal, J. D. Queen, Bill Gladden, Hinse Quinn, and Joe Ferebee; (third row) Jim Sadler, Burl Long, Dave Robinson, John Broome, Seller Edwards, and Sid Reep (manager). (Courtesy of Barry Long.)

An unidentified batboy for the Glenn Mills Red Devils sits with baseball equipment for this 1930s photograph. Games were played on mill property near the South Fork River, the present-day site of the Betty G. Ross Recreation Park. Members are, from left to right, (first row) unidentified, Edgar "Cap" Love, unidentified, and Clyde Lawing; (second row) C. R. Duncan (first baseman), Doc Rudisill, Jim Duncan, Harry Turner, and Burl Long. (Courtesy of Barry Long.)

Jay Shuford Boggs, in the center of the first row in this 1920s picture, served one year in the U.S. Navy and then enrolled at Lenoir-Rhyne College in Hickory, where he excelled in football, baseball, and basketball. He was voted Best All-Round Man in 1924. After college, he played Class-A ball in the Sally League and one year of professional baseball with the International League in Reading, Pennsylvania. His baseball career ended after he suffered severe sunstroke. (Courtesy of Polly Bryant.)

Representing the High Shoals community at the Lincoln–Gaston County border, the 1951 team includes, from left to right, (first row) Vernon "Moe" Cloninger, Rhett Doolittle, Paul Ballard, Jack Whitener, and Clyde "Dewberry" Heafner; (second row) Pervie Lineberger, Don Sullivan, Paul Baker, Frank "Ginny" Abernathy, Charles "Hussy" Huffsteller, and Jack Heafner. (Courtesy of Lynne C. Millwood.)

Lincolnton High graduate Russell "Red" Mincy played baseball under legendary Coach C. D. "Block" Smith. Upon graduation from high school in 1938, he started his professional baseball career in Huntington, West Virginia. Mincy left baseball to serve during World War II but resumed play for the naval air station team in Norfolk, Virginia. Mincy managed the Lincolnton Cardinals in 1948 and ended his career as the manager of the Marion Marauders. He coached a number of Lincolnton's Little League teams and was an avid golfer. (Courtesy of Leslie Costner.)

"Baby Ray" Cornwell captures two barefooted young men (right) as they peer into the camera anxiously awaiting the guest of honor—a donkey. On this evening in 1949, folks in Lincolnton held a donkey ball game as a local fund-raiser. Hauled into the stadium in a truck labeled "Donkey Ball—Tonite," the donkey provided more than just the entertainment. (LCMH.)

The Howell team of Cherryville (Gaston County) stands for a photograph in 1945, holding the title of Tri-County Champs. Team members from left to right are (first row) Harold Blackwood, Hugh Dellinger, J. B. Beam, Cecil Jenkins, Hugh Gaskay, and Ray Greene; (second row) Hense Quinn (manager), Hub Black, Lloyd Crane, Wayne Chapman, Ralph Connor, Alfred Brooks, Carroll Wright, and J. C. Brackett. An unidentified batboy sits on the first row. (Courtesy of Ralph Connor.)

On July 13, 1940, J. D. Queen and Fleta Ballard exchanged vows on home plate at Love Field before a baseball game between Boger and Crawford Mills and C.D.A. To assist the couple with their new life together, organizers pledged the game's net proceeds as a bridal gift. An estimated 2,000 people attended the ceremony and game. Organizers designated the evening's events "Queen Night." (Courtesy of Barry Long.)

"Chunk" Rudisill began his baseball career at Lincolnton High under C. D. "Block" Smith and was a standout in football and baseball for the Lenoir-Rhyne Bears. Rudisill is shown here in a Lincolnton Red Sox uniform. The Red Sox were affiliated with the Boston Red Sox before being purchased by the St. Louis Cardinals. Rudisill entered service in 1942 during his junior year at Lenoir-Rhyne as a member of the 82nd Airborne Division. He played professional baseball in Norfolk, Virginia, and Newark, New Jersey before coming back to Lincolnton in 1950 to manage the Lincolnton Cardinals. (Courtesy of Sally Rudisill.)

Ralph Connor played baseball for various teams in the Carolinas and was responsible for the organization of numerous leagues for the Recreation Department and Veterans of Foreign Wars (VFW) in Lincolnton. In July 1947, he organized a midget baseball team under the auspices of the Recreation Department. At Love field, Connor instructed boys aged 9 to 14 in batting and fielding fundamentals. The young men played teams from other communities, including Cherryville, Long Shoals, Wampum Mill, Boger and Crawford Mill, and Laboratory Mill. (Courtesy of Ralph Connor.)

Two unidentified Lincolnton Red Sox team members stand for *c.* 1947 photographs. On Saturday, April 26, 1947, the Red Sox took the field as a member of the Mid-State League, which included six other teams. Organizers, sports columnists, and reporters believed that the outstanding fielders and hitters increased the league play to the level of Class C or B. The Mid-State League held a full-time commissioner and secretary. Buck Mauney, former Lincolnton High and Lenoir-Rhyne College athlete, managed the Lincolnton Red Sox, and John Broome worked as the team's player-manager. Team members in the team's first year in the Mid-State League included as "Chunk" Rudisill (centerfielder), Forrest Caskey (pitcher), Reid Campbell (catcher and utility outfielder), Dewberry Heavner (first baseman and outfielder), Fred Withers (shortstop), John Broome (first baseman), J. R. Lineberger (left fielder), Buss Huffstetler (second baseman), Floyd Beal (catcher), J. H. Lineberger (third baseman), and Pete Crow (right fielder). (LCMH.)

"Bouncin' Bobby" Beal played second and third base for Lincolnton High, Cherryville Legion, Highland Park in Charlotte, Lincolnton Red Sox, Charlotte Hornets, Gadsden Pilots in Alabama, Lincolnton Cardinals, McDowell Indians in Marion, North Carolina, and a team in Greenville, South Carolina. He led the Hornets in 1947 with a .326 batting average. The Lincoln Cardinals hired him as a player-manager in 1951, and he led the team to a Western Carolina League pennant. After his playing career, he managed the Howard Furniture softball team. He was inducted into the Lincoln County Sports Hall of Fame in 2001. (Courtesy of Bob Beal Jr.)

HONORING THE MEMORY OF

COACH CHAS. D. "BLOCK" SMITH

Opening Game

LINCOLNTON CARDINALS
Vs.
NEWTON-CONOVER TWINS

★

Saturday Night, May 1st, 1948 — 8 O'clock
Lincolnton High School Park

In their first game in the Western Carolina League, the Lincolnton Cardinals honored Charles D. "Block" Smith (1901–1944) with a photograph on the program cover and a biographical sketch inside. Festivities included music from the Lincolnton High Band, a tribute to Coach Smith by Buck Mauney, and the throwing of the first ball by his wife, Elizabeth Johnson Hoke. Smith coached four men who participated in the game: D. H. Mauney Jr., owner of the Cardinals; Coley Gaffney; "Chunk" Rudisill; and Reid Caldwell. (Courtesy of Andy Mauney.)

At the end of World War II, North Carolina had 45 minor-league teams. The Lincolnton Cardinals, a popular team from 1947 through 1951 in the Western Carolina League, was owned by D. H. "Buck" Mauney Jr. Other stockholders were Joe Ross and Joe Polhill. The 1948 team, pennant winners and playoff champions, are, from left to right, (first row) Hal Abernethy, "Chunk" Rudisill, Junior Dodgin, Reid Campbell, Bobby Caldwell, and Judd Harmon; (second row) Fred Withers, Ben Pollock, J. R. Lineberger, Warren Richards, and Frank Richards; (third row) Marvin Mauney, Ernie Ibach, Bus Huffstetler, Jim Dodgin, and Red Mincy. (Courtesy of Andy Mauney.)

The Lincolnton Cardinals from the early 1950s wore the same uniforms as the 1948 team that won the league pennant with a record of 69-41. The Cardinals won the pennant after finishing a half-game ahead of Shelby with a record of 72-39 during the 1953 season. (Courtesy of Ralph Connor.)

John Henry Moss shakes hands with Buck Mauney after the Lincolnton Cardinals won the Western Carolina League Championship in 1948. Team members shown may include Bus Huffstetler, Fred Withers, and J. R. Lineberger. Lincolnton entered the Western Carolina League in 1948 and gave North Carolina 43 towns in organized baseball. In 1948, the Western Carolina League opened its 128-game schedule on April 30 and played the all-star game in Lincolnton on July 23. During the 1948 season, the league set a salary limit of $2,600, with a player limit of 17 that included three service veterans, seven class men, and seven rookies. (Courtesy of John Henry Moss.)

The Lincolnton Cardinals bus appears in this 1952 photograph of the winner and runner-up of the Miss Lincolnton Cardinal Pageant in 1952. Betty Wise was awarded the crown of Miss Lincolnton Cardinal, and Barbara Carter received the runner-up award. (Courtesy of Barry Long.)

Lincolnton photographer "Baby Ray" Cornwell visited the Glenn Mills community in Lincolnton to capture a team photograph *c.* 1947. The team members are, from left to right, (first row) Bobby Canipe, David Gardner, Maurice Carpenter, Bud Childers, Bob Buff, Harold Lawing, Larry Turner, and Bill Canipe (batboy); (second row) Donald Faulkenberry, Otha Jones, Wayne Carpenter, Sonny Turner, Charles Turner, Mack Canipe, and Lester Carter. Team coach Berlin Long is on the left in the third row. (Courtesy of Barry Long.)

The Carolina Mills team of Maiden (Catawba County) poses in an unidentified location in 1947. (LCMH.)

The Lincolnton American Legion Post 30 team, pictured in 1959, was Lincolnton's last official American Legion team before it became the Lincoln-Cherryville "Linc-Cherries." "Members are (front row) Buster Little, Barry Potts, unidentified, Worth Roberts, Bobby Beal, Don Cagle, and manager David "Chimp" Lynn; (second row) Chick Lineberger, Donnie Carrigan, Darrell Keener, David Lynn, Larry Seagle, Darrell Little, and Walt Cook; (third row) Jerry Dysart, Danny Ingle, Richard Smith, Clyde Ingle, and Coach Russell "Red" Mincy. (Courtesy of Leslie Costner.)

Richard Smith was a three-sport athlete at Lincolnton High during the early 1960s before playing professional baseball with the Washington Senators. After he retired from professional baseball, he returned to Lincolnton to follow in the footsteps of his former coach, Von Ray Harris. As football coach and athletic director at Lincolnton High, Smith coached the football team to a AA state championship in 1993, seven years after Harris's retirement. Smith's Wolves returned to the state championship the following year and were runners-up to Wallace–Rose Hill. (Courtesy of Richard Smith.)

During his freshman year at Lincolnton High, Steve Herman tossed 11 brilliant innings for the Lincolnton-Cherryville Legion team on the way to the Area 4 title over Shelby. Herman, as a six-foot-one-inch right-handed senior at Lincolnton High, pitched a no-hitter against Kings Mountain in 1963 and averaged two strikeouts per inning. He signed with the Philadelphia Phillies and played in the Western Carolina League with a team in Spartanburg. Lincolnton High baseball Coach Perry Brown is photographed with Steve Herman in this newspaper article from 1963. (Courtesy of Steve Herman.)

After Tony Cloninger from Iron Station missed out on a 1953 trip with the Cherryville American Legion team to Miami for the American Legion Series, he struck out 21 batters in an American Legion game against Charlotte. He signed a $100,000 contract with the Milwaukee Braves in 1958 and had a locker between Hank Aaron and Eddie Matthews. He was the Atlanta Braves' top winner in 1965, posting 24 victories. Cloninger retired in 1972. (LCMH.)

The 1953 Rock Springs High School baseball team won the Little 10 title, comprised of Gaston and Lincoln County teams, and the State Class A championship during their first conference year. Members include, from left to right, (first row) Ray Cloninger, Grady Barker, Junior Barkley, and Tommy Little; (second row) C. E. McCorkle, Herbert Loftin, Richard Sherrill, Walter Mundy, and Kermit Sigmon; (third row) Lester Ballard, Jimmy Mundy, Donald Miller, Murray Sherrill, and Coach W. T. Long. (LCMH.)

Coach Henry Barkley (top left) stands with players from East Lincoln High's first baseball team for the 1967–1968 season. Team members are, from left to right, (first row) Mike Goodson, Tony Loftin, Reid Schronce, Van Barker, unidentified, and Corky Mundy; (second row) Donnie Brown, Mike Summers, Butch Sigmon, Tom Lawing, unidentified, and Nelson Howard; (third row) Coach Henry Barkley, unidentified, Ricky Barker, Don Alexander, and two unidentified players. (Courtesy of Henry Barkley.)

Walter "Pooch" Cornwell was a three-sport athlete at Lincolnton High from 1949 to 1953. Cornwell excelled on the 1953 Cherryville Post 100 American Legion baseball team that played in the Little League World Series in Miami, Florida. At Lenoir-Rhyne College in Hickory, he earned all-conference and all-district honors in football, basketball, and baseball. The records he achieved still stand today. A sportswriter said, "The North State Conference and Lenoir-Rhyne College saw the end of one of the greatest . . . athletic careers in the state's history when Walter Cornwell bowed out." Cornwell was inducted into the Lincoln County Sports Hall of Fame in 2005. (LCSHF.)

The 1995 championship Lincolnton High baseball team posted a 26-3 record. Members are, from left to right, (first row) Bradley Clark (manager), Shane Roberson, Jonathan Brookins, Brian Blackwell, David Elliott, and Jessica Little (scorekeeper); (second row) Chad Mosteller (coach), Jamie Ewing, Marty Mincey, Cheron Farley, Brent Colvard, and Clay Sherrill; (third row) A. J. Henley (coach), Christ Wycoff, Jami Creech, Ron Colvard, Brett Carey, Dutch Leonard, Shane Sigmon, and Bobby Martin (coach). Members of the team not pictured are Cole Sigmon (coach), Trey Gilbert, Brandon Jones, Will Lane, John Mackie, Leigh Barnette (scorekeeper), and Jennifer Featherstone (scorekeeper). (Courtesy of Lincolnton High School.)

Jay Heafner pitched for West Lincoln High. As a four-year letterman, Heafner received All-Conference (three years), two-time All-Gaston Gazette Team, All-Gaston Area MVP, Gold Glove Award (2000), Best Hitter (2001), Best Defensive Player (2002), and MVP (2002) honors. At Davidson College in 2005, he ranked second in the country with a .448 batting average and set the record at Davidson College for pitching saves. The Texas Rangers drafted him in the 23rd round of the 2006 Major League Baseball draft. (Courtesy of Walt and Ann Heafner.)

At Davidson, Jay Heafner was Rookie of the Year in 2003, Co-MVP in 2004, and All–Southern Conference as a relief pitcher in 2004. In 2005, he was team MVP, All-State Team, All–Southern Conference, Southern Conference Player of the Year, All-American, Golden Spikes Award Watch List, and a Xanthus–Dick Howser Trophy nominee. The following year, Heafner was on the Brooks Wallace Award Watch List, served as team cocaptain, and was All–Southern Conference. He held records including first in pitching saves, second in hits, fourth in total bases, fourth in walks, fifth in runs scored, sixth in RBIs, and eighth in doubles. (Courtesy of Walt and Ann Heafner.)

Straddling the right and left field lines, members of North Lincoln High and Cherryville High take part in the dedication of lights at the new stadium with hats off for the national anthem. A fan stands atop the press box to capture this photograph in 2006. (Courtesy of Patty Skidmore.)

North Lincoln High's pitcher John Belk plans to deliver a strike at the game against Cherryville in 2006 after the dedication of the stadium lights. Graduating in 2006, Belk had a country record–breaking game against East Lincoln during the 2005–2006 season. (Courtesy of Patty Skidmore.)

During the 2003 season, the Cherryville North Carolina Post 100 reached the American Legion Word Series in Bartlesville, Oklahoma. Team members include Ben Lastra, Chris Halubka, Josh McSwain, Josh Glover, Jonathan Walker, Chris Mason, Evan Wise, Jay Heafner, David Wise, Matt Craig, Bobby Dale Reynolds (head coach), Travis Walls, Shane Summers, Steven Justice, Brock Alexander, Chuck Walker (assistant coach), Chris Cook, Jackson Beam, Wayne McDonald, Brandon Hurt, and A. J. Henley (assistant coach). (Courtesy of Don Wise.)

John "Cotton" Little of Rock Springs High in Denver signed a contract with the Cleveland Indians but remained in Lincoln County and eventually joined the military. Little competed in the Army World Series in Korea. He returned to Lincoln County and coached basketball with the county recreational program, Boger City Boosters, Boger City Methodist Church softball league, and the Catawba-Lincoln semi-professional baseball league. He was inducted into the Lincoln County Sports Hall of Fame in 2005. (Courtesy of Lincoln County Sports Hall of Fame.)

2

FOOTBALL

Though early photographs of football players and teams in Lincoln County only date from the early 1920s, various men from Lincoln County participated on football teams on the local and university level during the first two decades of the 20th century. As illustrated by a newspaper article and photograph of the "Gridiron Greats" from Lincoln County on page 35, young men organized teams that had only baseball uniforms to wear during their football games in the first decade of the 20th century. The members of these teams, as conveyed by Edgar "Cap" Love, traveled to surrounding counties in cars with light from kerosene lanterns. They wore pads that were not sufficient to prevent injuries, and their helmets were void of face masks that kept opposing players from puncturing the eyes and damaging the faces of players.

These early teams were the predecessors of organized football teams at local schools such as Lincolnton High under the tutelage of coaches such as Block Smith, Lyle Edwards, Von Ray Harris, Perry Brown, Richard Smith, and Scott Cloninger. Under these coaches, players such as "Chunk" Rudisill, Dennis Byrd, Steve Warren, Jerry Sain, and Mike Cline went on to play and achieve accolades at the collegiate level. The lessons learned from Lincoln County coaches pervaded their athletic careers. From the first conference champions at Lincolnton High in 1960 to the school's state championship team in 1993, many football players graduated from high school and college and returned to the county to give back to young men whose dreams rested in the hopes that their coaches would lead them in the same direction as their mentors.

Photographed in 1905 are Kemp Nixon and Trinity Football Team members including Whitley (left tackle–captain), Hide (fullback), Nixon (left guard), Groom (right end), Moses (left halfback), Brown (right tackle), Ross (center), Haywood (right halfback), Emerson (quarterback), Miller (left guard), Wrenn (right guard), Canon (left end), Lassiter (guard), Singletary (right guard), Gilmer (right end), and Perry (manager). (LCMH.)

Charles D. "Block" Smith sits second from left on the first row with his unidentified football team in 1921. (LCMH.)

On August 31, 1960, early Lincoln County athletes are photographed by Baby Ray Cornwell at the county courthouse. Joe B. Johnston, operator of Lincolnton's ice plant, recruited the "biggest and strongest young men in Lincolnton" for a game with Catawba College in 1907. The newly organized team only had baseball uniforms to wear for the game. Team members are, from left to right, Jim Shuford, Vaughan Padgett, Howard Leonard, Kemp Battle Nixon, and Frank Ramseur (seated). Members of the team not pictured were Bob Hinson, Barron F. Caldwell, Oscar Shuford, and Mason Pressley. (LCMH.)

The second year of football at Lincolnton High featured a stellar coaching performance by P. O. Bethea, star quarterback and halfback at Davidson College (1919–1920), and various players who played Catawba College to a 6-6 tie. Team members from 1923 include (identified predominately by last name): Royster, Yoder, V. Heavner, K. Heavner, Lohre, Beal, Kistler, Shuford, Howard, Jonas, Hoyle, Jenkins, Leonard, Harrill, Senter, L. Heavner, Huggins, Smith, J. Shuford, K. Goodson, G. Crowell, and K. Grigg. (LCMH.)

Coach Smith is pictured with the Lincolnton High football team in 1926. The team finished the season with a record of 6-2-1. Members include Edison Shuford, Bill Barineau, Bill Haynes, Kemp Huss, D. C. Leonard, Vivian Lackey, Victor Rudisill, Kenneth Dellinger, McCall Proctor, Ray Ward, Bill Goodson, Melvin Karesh, Carson Burke, Clay Beam, Elmer Burke, Paul Crowell, Forest Smith, Guy Rudisill, Kenneth Crowell, Urias Pierce, Ivey Johnson, and Fred Harrill. (LCMH.)

Hugh "Chunk" Rudisill wears a Lenoir-Rhyne football uniform in the 1930s. Rudisill played football and baseball at Lincolnton High and was a standout for the Boger and Crawford Mills and Lincolnton Red Sox baseball teams. Signed by the New York Yankees as a sophomore at Lenoir-Rhyne, Rudisill bypassed a professional career for World War II. Rudisill returned from the war and played for the Yankee's Class A farm team in Norfolk, Virginia. Later he played semi-professional baseball and served as a player-manager for the Lincolnton Cardinals in the early 1950s. (Courtesy of Sally Rudisill.)

Cecil "Brat" Stroup poses for photographer "Baby Ray" Cornwell around 1943. Brat carried the pigskin as tailback on offense and roamed the defensive side of the ball as a linebacker for Lincolnton High. He played in the 1944 Shrine Bowl, when North Carolina's team overtook an equally formidable team from South Carolina. He left for World War II in 1944 to serve in the Pacific on a destroyer escort. Upon returning to Lincolnton, Brat took a post-graduate class and played one more season of football. He was inducted into the Lincoln County Sports Hall of Fame in 2006. (LCMH.)

Jack Dellinger holds the football as Ralph Connor kicks a field goal during the 1941 season at Lincolnton High. Dellinger, Connor, and other members of Lincolnton High's football teams (1941–1943), including Coach Lyle Edwards, are the only surviving members of these teams. The surviving members meet twice a year for a few hours to reminisce about their experiences as athletes at Lincolnton High. (Courtesy of Jack Dellinger.)

Taken during the opening kickoff of a game at Lincolnton High's Love Field, this photograph shows the old Lincolnton Grammar School and the Lincolnton Wolves. During the 1941 season, the team boasted a 7-1-1 record and scored 128 points to their opponents' 32 points. In the photograph below, Jack Dellinger, Ralph Connor, and J. M. Broome are in their three-point stances for this photograph during the 1941 season. These three players, along with others such as Lee Elmore, Sam Freeman, Elliott Beal, Cecil "Brat" Stroup, and Clyde Knight, were part of the Lincolnton High football team (1941–1943). (Bottom image courtesy of Jack Dellinger.)

Lincolnton High School football players Jack Dellinger (left) and Ralph Connor pose in October 1945. During this time, F. D. "Jack" Kiser was the coach of the Lincolnton High Wolves. Both Dellinger and Connor returned to Lincolnton to participate in sports after serving during World War II. (Courtesy of Jack Dellinger.)

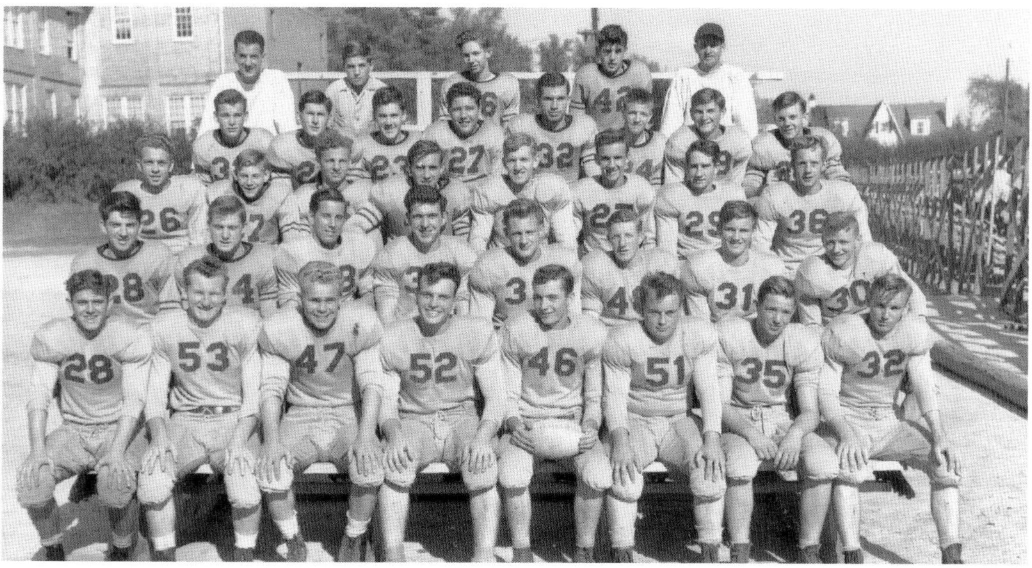

The 1946 Lincolnton High football team sit on the bleachers near Love field before their game against Rutherfordton-Spindale High on Monday, November 11, 1946. Team members include Harold Sain, Eugene Valentine, David Eaker, John Lawing, Paul Baker, Gus Finger, Jenky Leonard, George Burgin, Jennings Benfield, Paul Sisk, Bill Beattie, John Weaver, Brat Stroup, Jim Baab, Nelson Shrum, Steve Gabriel, Ransom Carpenter, Kennet Goodson, Junior Medlin, L. E. Rudisill, Bob Turner, Max Robinson, John McLean, Rathmul Helms, Mac Saunders, Bill Elliott, Bob Brackett, William Byers, Shirley Gabriel, Paul Peeler, Coach Troianio, Randolph Shives (manager), Kenneth Avery, Ed Leigh, and Jack Kiser (coach). (LCMH.)

Lincolnton High coaching legend Jack Kiser kneels with two of his players for a photograph during the 1947 football season. Lincolnton High School football cocaptains David Eaker (left) and Bill Beattie (right) await Coach Kiser's words of wisdom before a scrimmage game at Love Field. Eaker contributed to the team's strength as a lineman, and Beattie's ball-handling skills led the team's running attack. (LCMH.)

Paul "Blimpy" Haynes stands on the gridiron for this c. 1939 photograph. Haynes towered above his teammates at over six feet tall and well over 200 pounds. He exited the bus first during away games so that he could intimidate the opponents. Haynes's size was attributed to plenty of milk, cornbread, and ice cream. Upon completion of his athletic career, he went to work at his father's dairy in Lincolnton, which his son and grandsons still operate. (Courtesy of Paul Haynes.)

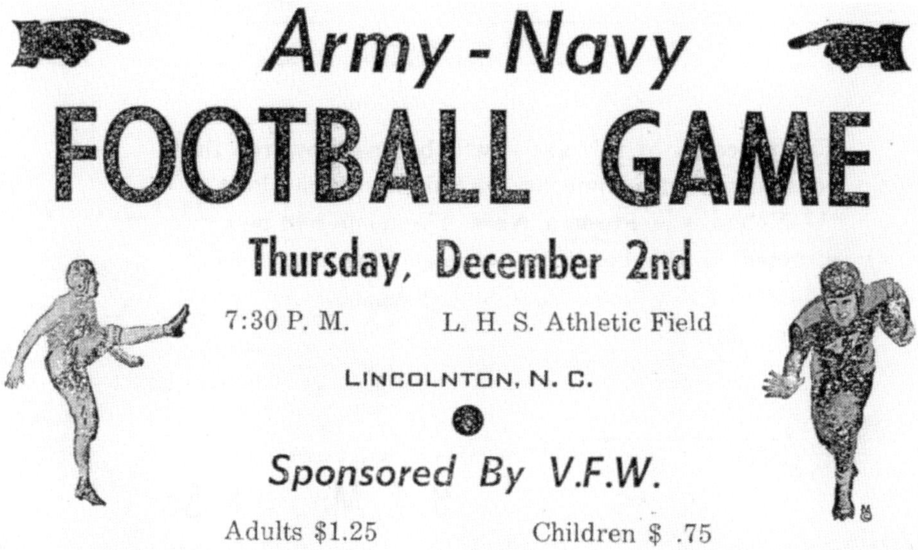

On December 2, 1948, a memorable game took place at Lincolnton High's field. Sponsored by the Shipp-Lockman VFW Post in Lincolnton, the game featured Lincoln County veterans of the army, air force, and marines against men from the navy and coast guard. Rain and mud did not stop the navy team from outlasting the army team in a 7-6 decision. Players included Lincoln County Sports Hall of Fame inductees "Chunk" Rudisill, Jule Ward, and Brat Stroup, coached by D. H. "Buck" Mauney and Ralph Connor. (LCMH.)

David Hunter "Buck" Mauney poses as a Lenoir-Rhyne Bear around 1933. Mauney (1913–1985) played football and baseball at Lincolnton High. He played tailback for the Bears from 1931 to 1935 and entered the University of North Carolina in 1936. He played football during the fall and during the spring worked at the Long Shoals Cotton Mill. Between 1935 and 1936, Mauney went to the Baltimore Colts training camp. In 1936, he formed the Carolina Amateur Football Association, composed of the Lincolnton All-Stars, Limestone Mills (Gaffney, South Carolina), Charlotte Bulldogs, and Mooresville Moore. In 1942, Mauney enlisted in the U.S. Navy. In 1948, he formed and owned the Lincolnton Cardinals. (Courtesy of Andy Mauney.)

Von Ray Harris built a strong football program at Lincolnton High. Harris took over the football program in 1959 and guided the team for over 20 years. Before retiring in 1987, Harris racked up a career coaching record of 246-133-9 and was a recipient of the North Carolina High School Athletic Directors Association Award in 1986. As the leader of the Wolves, he compiled a record of 185-97-8. He coached players that became high school football coaches, including Richard Smith, who took over Lincolnton High when Harris retired and won a state championship in 1993. Von Ray Harris was inducted into the Lincoln County Sports Hall of Fame in 2001. (LCSHF.)

Joseph Walter Harper III served as coach at Newbold High, one of Lincoln County's African American schools, which served grade 1 through 12 from 1956 to 1968. Harper compiled a football record of 75-29. His teams originally played six-man football and won the Western Division Six-Man Championship in 1956 and 1957. Harper's basketball teams compiled a record of 186-52. He received the Coach of the Year award from the Western Division of the North Carolina High School Athletic Association for football in 1966 and for basketball in 1967. He was inducted into the Lincoln County Sports Hall of Fame in 2002. (Courtesy of the Lincoln County Sports Hall of Fame.)

The Lincolnton High Wolves boasted a 9-1-1 record during the 1961 season and were champs of the Southwestern AAA Conference. From left to right are (first row) Ronnie Harris, Tony Darnell, Billy Williams, Eddie Hovis, Bobby Beal, Guy Howell, Harold Billings, Don Powers, Fred Alexander, and Richard Moody; (second row) Richard Smith, Curtis Beal, Nelson Beam, Robert Hawkins, Jerry Barkley, Ted Eurey, Billy Williams, Gary Richard, Don James, and Roby Jetton; (third row) Eddie Heavner, Jeff Turner, Andy Mauney, James Hoyle, David Ramseur, Buster Little, John Froneberger, Ralph Smith, George Page, and Jim Fortenbury; (fourth row) coaches Roy Turbyfill and Von Ray Harris. (Courtesy of Bobby Beal.)

Roby Jetton wore numerous athletic uniforms over the years. As tough as nails, he played football at Lincolnton High during the late 1950s and early 1960s and played two years beyond high school for the Gaston Patriots. He was a member of the 1961 Lincolnton High football team that went 9-1-1 and won the Southwestern AAA Conference Championship. While at Lincolnton High, Jetton was named to the All-Conference team and received an honorable mention on the All-State team. He is best known locally for his accomplishments in boxing. Jetton was inducted into the Lincoln County Sports Hall of Fame in 2003. (Courtesy of Roby Jetton.)

West Lincoln High offensive back Wesley D. Beam provides a stiff arm for the camera during the 1967 football season. Beam played football, baseball, and basketball for four years at West Lincoln and received All-Conference awards in football and baseball. He attended Appalachian State University, where he played as cornerback from 1968 to 1972. At West Lincoln, he coached defense for 8 years and was head football coach for 6 years, head baseball coach for 15 years, and athletic director for 6 years. He was named Coach of the Year in baseball for the Southwestern District 7 AA Conference in 1982–1983. He served as East Lincoln High's defensive coordinator for 13 years. He was inducted into the Lincoln County Sports Hall of Fame in 2003. (Courtesy of Wesley D. Beam.)

Lincoln County football legend Dennis Byrd was a standout lineman at Lincolnton High. Under Von Ray Harris, Don Pack, and Roy Turbyfill, Byrd received All–Southwestern Conference honors three years in a row. The City of Lincolnton held a "Dennis Byrd Night" for Lincolnton's first All-American football player and presented him the key to the city. He was also a member of the basketball team, and in four years as center, Byrd scored over 1,000 points. He was inducted into the Lincoln County Sports Hall of Fame in 2002. (Courtesy of Paul and Jennifer Byrd.)

Dennis Byrd shows his usual strength and posture in this 1960s photograph. Byrd was an all-conference and all-state lineman at Lincolnton High and played in the Shrine Bowl. He was one of the top linemen in the nation while at North Carolina State and earned three All–Atlantic Coast Conference (ACC) selections, two Coaches All-American selections, and was on the Kodak and Playboy All-American teams. The Boston Patriots drafted Byrd in the first round of the 1968 NFL draft with the sixth overall pick. His career was cut short because of knee problems. (Courtesy of Paul and Jennifer Byrd.)

Dennis Byrd displays a confident smile at his home on Cedar Street in Lincolnton after being drafted in the first round of the 1968 NFL draft by the Boston Patriots. His wife, Paulette, sits to his right, and his parents, Leonard and Dot Byrd, sit to his left as their son takes the next step in an outstanding athletic career. (Courtesy of Paul and Jennifer Byrd.)

Paulette Stroup shows her school spirit as a cheerleader for Lincolnton High in 1963. Paulette was a senior in high school during the time of this photograph, taken in the old Lincolnton High ("Block" Smith) gymnasium on East Rhodes Street. After graduation, Paulette married Lincolnton's football standout Dennis Byrd. (Courtesy of Paul and Jennifer Byrd.)

The West Lincoln High School football team lines up for a team photograph during the 1966 season. (Courtesy of Wesley Beam.)

Jerry Sain runs toward the camera for this photograph while at the University of North Carolina. Sain is a graduate of West Lincoln High, where he was an All-Conference player for the Rebels. The University of North Carolina (UNC) gave him a full scholarship, and as an offensive lineman there, he was a member of the All-ACC team. He is the only West Lincoln High alumnus to receive this award. Under UNC coach Bill Dooley, Sain played in two bowl games. After graduating from UNC with a degree in English, Sain returned to Lincoln County to teach at West Lincoln High and serve as an assistant football coach. He is shown below in his Tarheel uniform warding off a University of Virginia Cavalier. Jerry Sain was inducted into the LCSHF in 2002. (LCSHF.)

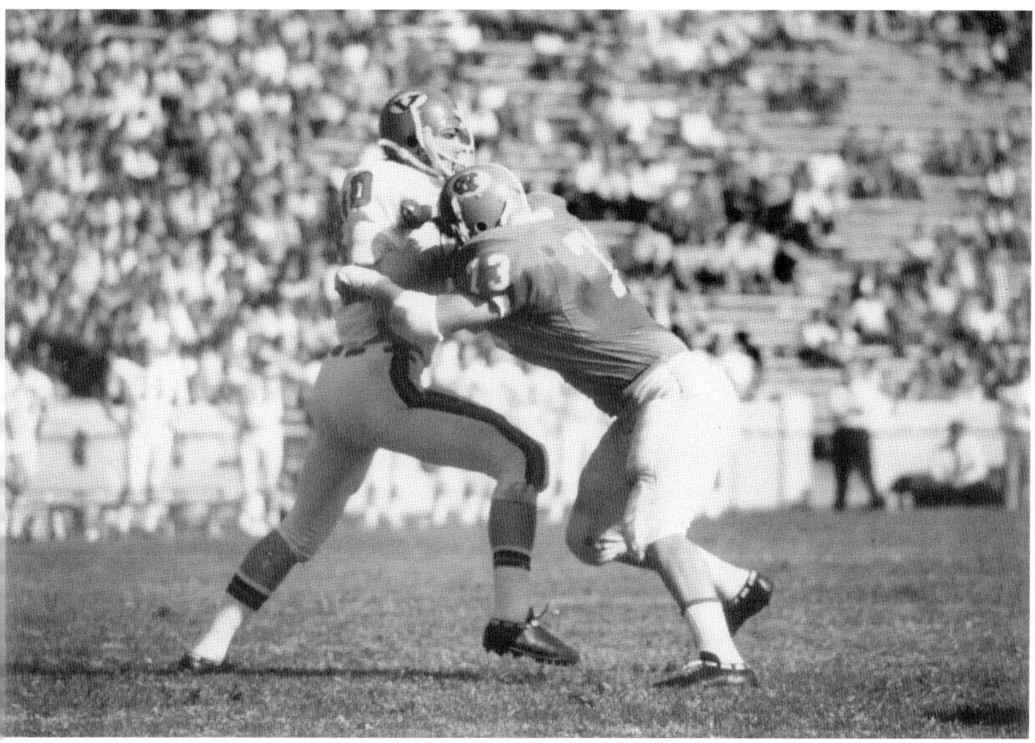

Mike "Cow" Cline (70) leads the charge of Lincolnton High's football team to set the tone for a 1969 game. The six-foot-one-inch, 235-pound lineman played three years (1966–1969) of varsity football at Lincolnton High School. He was cocaptain of the team during his senior year, made the All–Southwestern Conference Team, and received an honorable mention for the Greensboro *Daily News* all-state team. Along with his teammate Steve Arrington, Cline played college football at the University of South Carolina. (Courtesy of Mike and Libby Cline.)

Mike Cline proudly wears his uniform and a smile for this photograph while at the University of South Carolina from 1970 to 1974. During his freshman year, Cline played for the University of South Carolina Biddies before becoming a starting offensive lineman as an upperclassman. He received his varsity letter during his sophomore year. Upon completion of his college football career, Cline returned to Lincoln County and coached sports for East Lincoln High. (Courtesy of Mike and Libby Cline.)

Tommy Lawing stands ready to make a pass for this photograph during his tenure at East Lincoln High, where he was the first quarterback in 1967. He lettered in football, baseball, and basketball. He and his future wife, Annette Callaway, were part of the first fully integrated class at East Lincoln. Tommy graduated in 1969, and his son Todd carried on the family's football tradition at East Lincoln by playing quarterback. (LCMH.)

Annette Callaway proudly lifts her pom-poms as a cheerleader of East Lincoln High's first cheerleading team. The squad held try-outs on the first lawn of Rock Springs School in eastern Lincoln County. Callaway lettered as a cheerleader from 1967 to 1970 and as member of the basketball team during the 1968–1969 season. Callaway graduated in 1970 and married Tommy Lawing (photographed above) in 1972. All three of Tommy and Annette's sons—Michael, Todd, and Derek—became athletes at East Lincoln High. (LCMH.)

East Lincoln High has a reputable history of athletic programs that dates to the school's founding over 40 years ago. The football team was fortunate to have these coaches from the 1980s; from left to right are (first row) Mark Lackey, Wes Beam, and Bruce Bolick; (second row) Mike Harrill, James Herndon, and Jim Soesbee. (Courtesy of Wes Beam.)

Kelly Childers (1963–1966) played linebacker and halfback at Wake Forest for one year before injury. He graduated from UNC-Pembroke with a degree in physical education. He came home to North Brook (1970) and taught physical education for one year, then went to East Lincoln High School and coached junior-varsity basketball and football. He moved to West Lincoln in 1973 and was an assistant coach and junior varsity coach and head basketball coach until 1983. (Courtesy of Kelly Childers.)

Members of the 1979 East Lincoln High football team stand for this photograph after they received their trophies and recognition. Coach Mike Cline stands in the middle as Eric Reel and Mark Devine stand to his left. The two young men standing to the right of Coach Cline are unidentified. The Mustangs finished the 1979 season as District Champs. (Courtesy of Mike Cline.)

Lincolnton High won a state championship in 1993 with a record of 13-2. From left to right are (first row) Charles Briggs, Jeff Hovis, Tiyon Adams, Bryan Littlejohn, Brett Carey, Lacosta Torrence, Damien Luce, Corey Barnes, Latrelle McClain, Leon Bostic, and Ricardo Jimenez; (second row) Mike Briggs (coach), Matthew Mullen, Cheron Farley, Tyler Friday, Quincey Odom, Shannon McAfee, Andre Bess, Antwan Wyatt, D. J. Stover, Reco Friday, and Demetrik Wilson; (third row) Franklin Smith, Shannon Ramseur, Matthew Patton, Tim Howard, Quentin Abernathy, Joey Robinson, Kevin McLain, Ben Charles, Derrick High (manager), and Josh Kiser (manager); (fourth row) Richard Smith (coach), Eric Wise, Jeremy Rice, Brian Crisson, Josh Atkins, Jamie Bryant, Greg Huss, James Jimenez, Fredrico Madrigal, Shamaine Edwards (manager), and Fred Maye (trainer); (fifth row) Fred Dalrymple (trainer), Jonathan Reep, Matthew Mullen, B. J. Russ, Jamie Lynch, Joe King, Stan Brooks, Tommy Roberts, Walden Link, and A. J. Henley (coach); (sixth row) Bobby Martin (coach), Scott Cloninger (coach), Craig Kiser (coach), Jeremy Morrison, Anwar Wyatt, Dutch Leonard, Jonathan Peeler, Cole Sigmon (coach), and Michael Propst (coach). (Courtesy of Lincolnton High School.)

Team spirit should be the title of this undated photograph of a young boy and girl in Lincolnton High uniforms. Lincolnton boasts many teams and players that make up the social history of Lincoln County. Before athletic teams at the school, people organized teams that participated in events in adjoining towns. This long and established history of city and county sports continues today, as teams from all over the county draw fans to high school stadiums. (Courtesy of David Napier.)

Offensive back Wes Beam carries the ball for West Lincoln High during a game against Hildebran, now East Burke, around 1967. Carroll Shidal (32), Nick Goins (63), and Alan Boyles (75), all West Lincoln Rebels and teammates of Wes Beam, are part of the action. (Courtesy of Wesley Beam.)

3

BASKETBALL

One of the most outstanding, memorable, and formable athletic programs in Lincoln County over the past 60 has been basketball. Both men and women's teams across the county have won conference, tournament, district, and state championships. Under coaches such as Elizabeth Hoke, F. D. "Jack" Kiser, Joe Kiser, Norris Childers, and Henry Barkley, women's basketball teams at Lincolnton High, Union High, North Brook High, and East Lincoln High have achieved accolades featured in books, annuals, and trophies in homes of many women and men throughout the county.

F. D. "Jack" Kiser, coach and educator, established an unprecedented winning tradition at Lincolnton High that may never again be matched in the annals of Lincoln County sports history. During his tenure from 1945 to 1961, the women's basketball team had a record of 351-41-3, won 13 conference championships, and between 1944 and 1951 lost only once in 171 games. Norris Childers lead his North Brook High girls' basketball teams to a remarkable record of 156-26 from 1946 to 1953. Henry Barkley coached the East Lincoln High girls' basketball team and guided them to a AA state championship—the only state championship in school history—in 1973 with a flawless record of 30-0, cementing his place in the county sports hall of fame.

Young athletes such as Betty Ross, Shirley Moore, and Rantie Killian in Lincoln County received instruction from an early age from youth programs sponsored by the Lincolnton Recreation Department and Shipp-Lockman Post 1706 VFW, in addition to great coaches in the eastern and western parts of the county that introduced basketball to their youth. These coaches and mentors provided basketball players with instruction that would prepare them to excel in middle school, high school, and college athletics.

Hugh Jenkins hugs a basketball that bears the writing: "1st LHS" for Lincolnton High School during the 1921–1922 season. Team members are, from left to right, Graydon Shuford, Hugh Jenkins, Howell Gabriel, Lemuel Wetmore, Edgar Love, and Sidney McCutcheon. (LCMH.)

The Lincolnton High boys' basketball team stands in formation at an outdoor court in 1923. They boasted a record of 13-6 during the season and were handicapped "because of the lack of an indoor court on which to play and practice, being forced to play several games on such courts," according to the yearbook. Team members and their positions include Kenneth Goodson (forward), Harry Wyckoff (forward), Alton Wood (forward), Edwin Royster (forward), Murl Huggins (center), Donald Jonas (guard), Hugh Jenkins (guard), James Smith (guard), Thomas Harrill (guard), and H. F. Krauss (coach). (LCMH.)

The Lincolnton High boys' basketball team sits on the steps of the school with their socks rolled down in black sneakers for this photograph in 1929. Coach "Block" Smith and managers Victor Rudisill and Harmon James are pictured with the following players: (not listed in order) Paul Bangle, Hunter Mauney (captain), Willie Ramsey, Marshall Brown, Gordon Goodson, Jack Costner, Frank Heavner, Poley Hauss, Johnnie Johnson, Jesse Robinson, Ralph Yoder, William Ridenhour, Claude Bynum, Robert Allison, and Fred Rudisill. (LCMH.)

In contrast to the black sneakers of the boys' team, the girls of the Lincolnton High School basketball team wear white sneakers for their team photograph to commemorate the 1929 season. Elizabeth Hoke sits proudly at the top right of the photograph with team managers Victor Rudisill and Harmon James. Members of the 1929 team include Wilma Ramsey, Lucille Lineberger, Ruth Leonard, Elizabeth Shuford, Laura Combs, Nell Sharpe, Frances Mauney, Leonora Gamble, Virginia Hoyle, Mildred Hovis, Ethelene McGinnis, Mary Bandy, and Erleen Padgett. (LCMH.)

Coach Elizabeth Hoke smiles as she holds the team ball during the 1930 basketball season at Lincolnton High. Though all of the players are not included in this photograph, they are identified by position, as follows: (forwards) Julia Schronce, Ruth Leonard, Wilma Ramsey, Jane Costner, Elizabeth Shuford, Nell Barlow, Sarah Reinhardt, Mattie Bishop, and Aline Rudisill; (guards) Mary Frances Shuford, Martha Haynes, Leanora Gamble, Margaret Honeycutt, Helen Childers, Mary Bandy, Sarah Padgett, and Elizabeth Barineau. (LCMH.)

The girls of the Iron Station basketball team sit on the steps of their school for this 1931 photograph. From left to right, the girls, with their nicknames, and coach are (first row) Bertha Ewing (Bert), Gladys Ewing (Dot), Ethel McClure (Cutie or Sparkie), and Ruth Ewing (Pete); (second row) Coach V. G. Shuford, Sue Betty Proctor (Pally), Wilvie Ewing (Runt), Lattie Long (Nick), and Mabel Ruth Sherrill (Babe). (Courtesy of David Napier.)

The Lincolnton High School boys' basketball team sits outside their high school building for this 1931 yearbook photograph. Members of the team are "Buck" Mauney, J. C. Burke, John Broome, Willie Ramsey, Ralph Yoder, Buck Goodson, Quilmer Fortenbury, Jesse Robinson, Fred Rudisill, and Loy D. Elmore. Coach C. D. "Block" Smith sits at the far left on the front row. (Courtesy of LCMH.)

Fred McCall Jr. holds a basketball that tells the story of Rock Springs High School's 1939–1940 season: "Champs, W.N.C." Team members include, from left to right, (first row) Harry Graham, Rodney Sherrill, Grady Howard, Fred McCall Jr., Harven Crouse, Ab Lynch, and Olen Painter; (second row) Kenneth Jetton, Harold Howard, Horace Crouse, J. W. Sigmon, and L. G. McCall; (third row) Bill Ballard, Coach Amendela, Howard Long, Hugh Duckworth, Aumon Sherrill, and Vaness Barker. (LCMH.)

Coach Kiser wears his academic sweater and tie for this 1947 photograph of the Love Memorial School's boys' basketball team. The boys are, from left to right: (first row) Max Canipe, Jack Benfield, Charles Snipes, Benny Hoyle, and Don Fortenberry; (second row) Floyd Williams, Kenneth Buff, Coach Ralph Kiser, Harold Gilbert, Carl Detter, and Dennis Young. (LCMH.)

With the basketball court in the background, principal Carl Ayers stands with his girls' basketball team at Love Memorial School in Lincolnton in 1947. The members are, from left to right: (first row) Doris Mace, Billie Dysart, Betty Hughes, Hazel Caldwell, and Edith Carpenter; (second row) Margie Whisnant, Mildred Wiggins, Coach J. C. Ayers, Phyllis Mauney, and Hattie Sutton. (LCMH.)

An unidentified coach, far right, stands with his Lincolnton semi-professional basketball team for this photograph in the 1940s. The team includes, from left to right, (first row) Betty Proctor, Helen Warren, Betty Biggerstaff, Sue Beattie, Wilhelmina Reynolds, and Geneva Painter; (second row) Helen Sellers, Reba Anthony, Thelma Caswell, Betty Gabriel, and ? Ewing. (Courtesy of Betty G. Ross.)

The 1940 Lincolnton High girls' basketball team poses as conference champions. Team members include Inez Dellinger, Betty Gabriel, Sue Beattie, Kate Ewing, Polly Miller, Irene Robinson, Martha Jean Caskey, Gladys Hayes, Louise Devine, Katherine Beam, Martha Bradshaw, Louise Ballard, Ester Ann Mullen, Elsie Summey, Katherine Sigmon, Ruth Parker, Katherine Devine, Hester Helms, Ruth Heavner, Willene Miller, Frances Moore, Cornelia Perkins, Teeny Dellinger, Ava Lee Grayson, Essie Wilson, Helen Ross, and Roxanne Lynch. (Courtesy of Betty G. Ross.)

The Lincolnton High boy's basketball team poses for this "Baby Ray" Cornwell photograph around 1942. Team members are, from left to right, (first row) Bill Chapman, Ray Reinhardt, Charles Gabriel, Jack Yoder, Wade Dodgin, and Paul Gabriel; (second row) Donald Clanton, Bill Yoder, Garmon Shrum, Buster Knight, and Oscar Elmore; (third row) managers Junior Seagle and Cecil "Brat" Stroup. (LCMH.)

Betty Gabriel Ross stands in a defensive position for this early-1940s photograph. Betty played four years of varsity basketball at Lincolnton High and was a multi-sport athlete at Appalachian State University. She became the director of the recreation department in Lincolnton in 1947 and witnessed its growth and development over 60 years. In 1977, Lincolnton built the South Fork Recreation Park with funds from a government grant and the Timken Foundation. During the 1990s, city fathers named the park in Ross's honor. Ross was inducted into the Lincoln County Sports Hall of Fame in 2001. (Courtesy of the Lincoln County Sports Hall of Fame.)

The Lincolnton High boys' basketball team congregated on the school steps for this 1944 photograph. Team members are, from left to right, (first row) Oscar Elmore, Bill Elmore, Charlie Gabriel, John Hugh Weaver, and Garmon Shrum; (second row) Jack Harvell, Sam Burgin, Ralph Carpenter, and Edward Killian; (third row) Coach Jack Kiser, ? Bogg, Ted Corriher, Doyle Bynum, and Cecil Stroup. (LCMH.)

"Baby Ray" Cornwell is able to catch a few members of the Lincolnton High boys' basketball team for this 1940s shot. Pictured from left to right are Jim Babb, unidentified, Jennings Benfield, Gene Ross, ? Cohen, and Steve Grabriel (seated). (LCMH.)

The ladies of the Lincolnton High girls' basketball team take a time-out for this photograph at their 1940s tournament. Photographed from left to right are (first row) Betty Sue Ellis, Frances Angle, Bobbi Lockman, Rachel Coffey, Nancy Kiser, Romona Heavner, Betty Heavner, and Betty Reynolds; (second row) Gloria Hallman, Peggy Caskey, unidentified, Gloria Hovis, Winnon Lineberger, Joanne Huffstetler, unidentified, Dorothy Dellinger, and Barbara Carter; (third row) Betty Wise, Bernice McCurry, Faye Bost, Daphine Johnson, unidentified, and Beth Cornwell. (LCMH.)

The Lincolnton High girls' basketball team of 1942 chooses not to hold the ball for the team's photograph on the school steps. They are, from left to right, (first row) Helen Hallman, Betty Gabriel, Louise Devine, and Sue Baity; (second row) Helen Ross and Betty Biggerstaff. (LCMH.)

Billy Joe Cornwell holds the basketball for the Lincolnton High boys' basketball team photograph in 1948. Team members include (first row) Shirley Gabriel, Paul Baker, Billy Joe Cornwell, Steve Gabriel, and Bill Beattie; (second row) Jim Baab, John Lowder, Neil Finger, and Bob Keener; (third row) Dan Reynolds, Randolph Shives, and Coach A. M. Troianio. (LCMH.)

The Lincolnton High girls' basketball team sports their slick uniforms for a photograph during the 1948 basketball season. Coach Floyd David "Jack" Kiser stands on the school steps for this photograph with his team, including Betty Lawing (34), Faye Bost (16), Betty Craig (with ball), Carolyn Johnson Howard (1), Pat Cagle Rudisill (2), Beth Cornwell (12), Naomi Canipe (in jacket), Betty Wise (15), Helen Anthony (second from last), Myra Gardner (18), Elizabeth Fergis, Bernice McCurry, Daphine Johnson, Pat Shuford, Peggy Caskey, and Doris Rice. (LCMH.)

Coach Kiser stands with one of his many championship teams for this 1952 photograph, which was made to mount on the championship trophy. Other folks who accompanied the team to the state tournament in Southern Pines included Mrs. Charles D. "Block" Smith and L. David Warlick. The team defeated Clarkton 75-47 to get to the state championship and eventually won the title. (LCMH.)

Coach Kiser (1906–1993) was an athlete at Lenoir-Rhyne, playing football, basketball, and baseball. He was named to the Lenoir-Rhyne College Sports Hall of Fame in 1979. After graduating in 1930, he coached Cherryville High School. From 1943 to 1945, Kiser coached at Bessemer City High School. In 1945, he came to Lincolnton to be coach and principal of Lincolnton High, a position he held until 1970. His Lincolnton teams captured 13 conference titles, 8 conference tournaments, and 2 state championships. His record for girls' basketball was 236-15, and he was inducted into the Lincoln County Sports Hall of Fame in 2001. (LCMH.)

The Rock Springs girls' basketball team huddles together in this 1950s team photograph. The players include, from left to right, (first row) two unidentified girls, Frances Mundy, Dolly Hager, and unidentified; (second row) Merle Joy Black, Barbara Little, Jane ?, Shirley ?, Elizabeth ?, and Betty Little. (LCMH.)

Norris Childers was one of the most successful coaches in Lincoln County history. From 1946 to 1953, Childers led North Brook High's girls' baseball teams to a record of 156-26, going undefeated at home. The team won a number of championships. He helped girls' basketball become an important and respected varsity sport during the 1940s and 1950s. Childers played for the Cherryville Legion team in 1934–1935. He graduated from North Brook High in 1936 and was a four-year starter for Lenoir-Rhyne. He served with the army during World War II. Norris Childers was inducted into the LCSHF in 2001. (Courtesy of Kelly Childers.)

The North Brook High boys' basketball team poses for a photograph during the late 1940s at the Western Gold Medal High School Basketball Tournament in Valdese, North Carolina. The team members are, from left to right, (first row) Pate Brendle, Buck Warlick, Paul Anthony, Charles Biggerstaff, and Junior Brendle; (second row) Bud Beam, Norman Young, Coach Norris Childers, Robert Hoyle, Kermit Lackey, and Robert Leonhardt. (Courtesy of Kelly Childers.)

The North Brook Blue Jays circle the ball in their gymnasium in western Lincoln County for this 1950s photograph. Pictured from left to right are Junior Brendle, Pate Brendle, Norman Young, Buck Warlick, Coach Norris Childers, Kermit Lackey, Paul Anthony, Charles Biggerstaff, Bobby Mosteller, Robert Hoyle, Robert Leonhardt, and Bud Beam. (Courtesy of Kelly Childers.)

In 1950, the Blue Jays made one of many appearances in the Western High School Basketball Tournament in Valdese, North Carolina. Team members include, from left to right, (first row) Bud Beam, Pate Brendle, Robert Leonhardt, John Beam Jr., and Max Tallent; (second row) Bobby Mosteller (manager), Max Wilkinson, Buck Warlick, Charles Biggerstaff, Paul Anthony, Norman Young, and Coach Norris Childers. (Courtesy of Kelly Childers.)

Coach Norris Childers stands in front of a capacity crowd during an award ceremony at North Brook High during the 1950s. In addition to the individual trophies that the staff presented to the players, a larger trophy sits on the table behind the group awaiting the team presentation. (Courtesy of Kelly Childers.)

Coach Childers was a very successful coach at North Brook High, not only with his boys' basketball teams, but also with his girls' teams. The girls are, from left to right, (first row) Sadie Newton, Shirlene Houser, Betty Jo Boyles, Ida Boyles, Dot Hoyle, and Guyanne Hull; (second row) Juanita Houser, Christine Boyles, Dorcus Sain, Daisy Leatherman, and Faye Hoyle; (third row) Doris Boyles, Gertie Bess, Justine Lingerfelt, Coleen Warlick, Mary Helms, Grace Willis, Joan Sain, and Betty Sain; (fourth row) Coleen Beam (manager), and Norris Childers (coach). (Courtesy of Kelly Childers.)

Juanita Houser holds another championship trophy won by the North Brook High girls' basketball team during the 1950s. Team members are, from left to right, (first row) Agness Bess, Faye Hoyle, Anne Beam, Nadine Houser, Juanita Houser, Dorcus Sain, Frances Willis, and Vida Sue Lingerfelt; (second row) Beverley Jane Heavner, Kaye Houser, Peggy Boyles, Floann Brendle, Charlene Houser, Jearlene Boyles, Jean Canipe, Lessie Prue Sain, unidentified, and coach Norris Childers. (Courtesy of Kelly Childers.)

The North Brook High girls' basketball team has their team photograph taken in the gym during the 1950s. The girls are, from left to right, (first row) Justina Lingerfelt, Dorcus Sain, Juanita Houser, and Joanne Sain; (second row) Peggy Sue Houser, Betty Sain, Mary Beth Houser, and Faye Hoyle; (third row) Betty Joe Parker and Faye Sain. Beverly Jane Heavner (manager) sits with the girls on the left, and coach Norris Childers sits proudly to the right of the team. (Courtesy of Kelly Childers.)

The 1950 girls' basketball team from North Brook High attended the Western High School Basketball Tournament in Valdese. Team members are, from left to right, (first row) Beverly Jane Heavner (manager), Christine Boyles, Mary Beth Houser, Betty Sain, Joanne Sain, Juanita Houser, and Betty Jean Bess; (second row) Dorcus Sain, Elizabeth Houser, Justina Lingerfelt, Doris Upton, Shirlene Houser, Guyann Hull, and coach Norris Childers. (Courtesy of Kelly Childers.)

The North Brook High girls' basketball team forms a circle at half court for this 1950s team photograph. Team members are, from left to right, Faye Hoyle, Juanita Houser, Betty Jo Boyles, Daisy Leatherman, Ida Boyles, Guyanne Hull, Shirlene Houser, Sadie Newton, Christine Boyles, Dorcus Sain, and unidentified. Manager Coleen Beam and coach Norris Childers overlook the group during the photograph. (Courtesy of Kelly Childers.)

Two members of the North Brook High girls' basketball team stand ready to defend or steal the basketball from an unfortunate member of the opposing team during a game in the 1950s. (Courtesy of Kelly Childers.)

Wes Beam, athletic standout at West Lincoln High and Appalachian State University, takes a jump shot with Ferrell Self behind him awaiting a potential rebound during a game against Granite Falls during the 1967–1968 season. (Courtesy of Wesley D. Beam.)

The Lincolnton High boys' varsity basketball team stands without regard for the three-second rule for this photograph from the 1960–1961 season. Team members include, from left to right, Harold Billings, Johnny Carpenter, Don Powers, Junior Norman, Richard Smith, Tommy Thompson, Bobby Beal, Fred Alexander, and Guy Howell. Coach Von Ray Harris and managers, Bobby Stamey and Tony Darnell, take a knee for the photograph. John Froneberger, Dennis Byrd, and Jim Fortenberry are not included in the photograph. (Courtesy of Bobby Beal.)

Bobby Beal takes a jump shot for this photograph in 1960. Beal, the son of a professional baseball player, was a member of the Lincolnton High football team that won the Southwestern Conference title in 1961. Beal attended North Carolina State University and upon graduation returned to Lincolnton to be involved with athletics as a softball player and coach of youth baseball, basketball, and football. In 1988, he received from Rotary International the Award for Coaching Dedication and Service to Youth. (Courtesy of Bobby Beal.)

The East Lincoln High women's basketball team sported a 23-2 record during the 1969–1970 season and finished the season as conference and district champions. Pictured are, from left to right, (first row) Marcella McLean, Gail Ballard, Elaine Elliott, Dianne Painter, Virginia Cherry, Patsy Helton, and manager Kathy Ballard; (second row) Becky Caskey, Malynda Cherry, Sandy Robinson, Coach Henry Barkley, Vicki Grigg, Patti Ewing, and Dayle Howard. (Courtesy of Henry Barkley.)

Marcella McLean poses in a defensive stance for this photograph in the East Lincoln High Gymnasium for the 1969–1970 season. As one of the first African American women that participated in women's sports at East Lincoln High, McLean received All-Conference honors from 1968 to 1970 under Coach Henry Barkley. (Courtesy of Henry Barkley.)

Whether taking a shot from the free-throw line or a jump shot from the baseline over a member of the opposing team, Rantie Killian dominated high school basketball in Lincoln County. Killian was a member of East Lincoln High's girls' basketball team that won the state championship and is the top scorer in school history. (Courtesy of Henry Barkley.)

Brenda Johnson Hamilton holds the tool that led her and the 1973 East Lincoln girls' basketball team to a state AA championship—the only state title won by the school. Johnson was All-Conference (1971–1973), Most Valuable Player Southern District (1971–1973), and All-State (1971–1973). Hamilton holds a scoring record at East Lincoln High with 41 points in one game. Upon graduation, Hamilton played women's basketball at Western Carolina University in Coolemee and has coached youth basketball in Lincoln County. She was inducted into the Lincoln County Sports Hall of Fame in 2005. (Courtesy of Henry Barkley.)

Henry Barkley participated in baseball and basketball at Rock Springs High and at Lenoir-Rhyne. He was a member of the Rock Springs baseball team that won a state championship in 1953. He returned to eastern Lincoln County to coach baseball, football, and basketball at Rock Springs High. He moved to East Lincoln High during the 1960s and served as the head baseball coach, golf coach, assistant football coach, girls' basketball coach, and athletic director. He was inducted into the Lincoln County Sports Hall of Fame in 2002. (Courtesy of the Lincoln County Sports Hall of Fame.)

Coach Henry Barkley stands proudly in front of the 1972–1973 East Lincoln girls' basketball state champions. It was with this and other girls' basketball teams at East Lincoln that Coach Barkley built a reputable and memorable tradition. Barkley's 1973 team won the state AA championship with an impeccable 30-0 record. In 1987–1988, Lincoln County awarded him the honor of Principal of the Year. (Courtesy of the Lincoln County Sports Hall of Fame.)

East Lincoln women's basketball standout Rantie Killian lays the ball in the basket over an opposing defender during this photograph from the early 1970s. Under Coach Henry Barkley, the East Lincoln girls' basketball team accumulated an outstanding record that continued the women's basketball tradition established during the 1940s and 1950s by such coaches as Jack Kiser and Norris Childers. (Courtesy of Henry Barkley.)

Sheila Barker stands ready to shoot or make a pass at half court in the East Lincoln High School gymnasium for this photograph during the early 1970s. Barker and other member of the Mustangs women's basketball team received numerous awards during the early 1970s and won a state championship during the 1972–1973 season. (Courtesy of Henry Barkley.)

Patti Ewing handles the ball for the East Lincoln High girls' basketball team. Ewing received numerous honors during her athletic career as a forward for the Mustangs, including All-Conference honors during the 1970–1971 and 1971–1972 seasons, and was voted Most Valuable Player in Southern District 7 during the 1970–1971 season. (Courtesy of Henry Barkley.)

Jamye Barkley stands at half court ready to add another assist to her record. Barkley, whose father is Coach Henry Barkley, played for the East Lincoln High girls' basketball team from 1979 to 1981. During her career at East Lincoln, Jamye was the county assist leader. (Courtesy of Henry Barkley.)

Twins Julia and Jane Heavner hold the basketball in place for this photograph during Union High's 1956–1957 season. Members of the team include Alice Mosteller, Kay Smith, Jane Heavner, Julia Heavner, Betty Abernethy, Clarice Smith, Margaret Leatherman, Vertie Sue King, Earlene Sain, Faye Hoyle, Carolyn Houser, and Wilma Canipe. Coach Joe Kiser stands to the right of the group, and Linda Royster was the team's manager. (LCMH.)

The Union High yearbook, the *Acorn*, featured this photograph of the boys' basketball team in 1958. Coach Joe Kiser stands in his suit to the right of the group as they wear their warm-up sweats. Members of the team include Clyde Ingle, M. D. Morgan, Yates Reep, Jack Sain, Ralph Warlick, Dougles Ledford, Steve Carpenter, Franklin Scronce, and Troy Scronce. Jerry Scronce was absent for the yearbook photograph. Tommy Rhyne and David Warlick were managers for the 1958 team. (LCMH.)

4

Boxing

Boxing in Lincoln County began with the implementation of the program at Lincolnton High in the 1920s. The outgrowth of this program and other programs was predicated by the work of Arnold "Jersey" Tarr when he came to Lincolnton during the 1930s. Tarr came to Lincoln County and worked at Cochrane Furniture Company. Tarr trained a number of boxers during the 1930s who eventually went on to box at Lincolnton High. Many of these boxers and later boxers participated in training events that did not include the leadership of an instructor but encompassed the organization of young men that assembled themselves locally to train outside the bounds of organized boxing. They assembled themselves in the basement of Lincolnton High to train and prepare for the Golden Gloves Tournament in Gastonia or Charlotte.

Later programs at the Shipp-Lockman No. 1706 VFW and Lincolnton Recreation Department in Lincolnton, headed by men such as Ralph Connor and Ken "Chick" McCurry, prepared men such as Jim Carter, Sonny Taylor, Lee Boyd, David McCullough, Roby Jetton, and Billy Bridges to win many titles that further established and advanced the boxing program in Lincoln County. Men such as Connor and McCurry worked incessantly to build the careers of young men from Lincoln County to achieve goals including Junior Olympics titles, Golden Gloves championships, and the World Boxing championships.

Three bare-fisted fighters from the Lincolnton High boxing team display a menacing growl in front of the school for this 1940s photograph. The boxing team members are unidentified, Bill Millburn, and Walter Lineberger. (LCMH.)

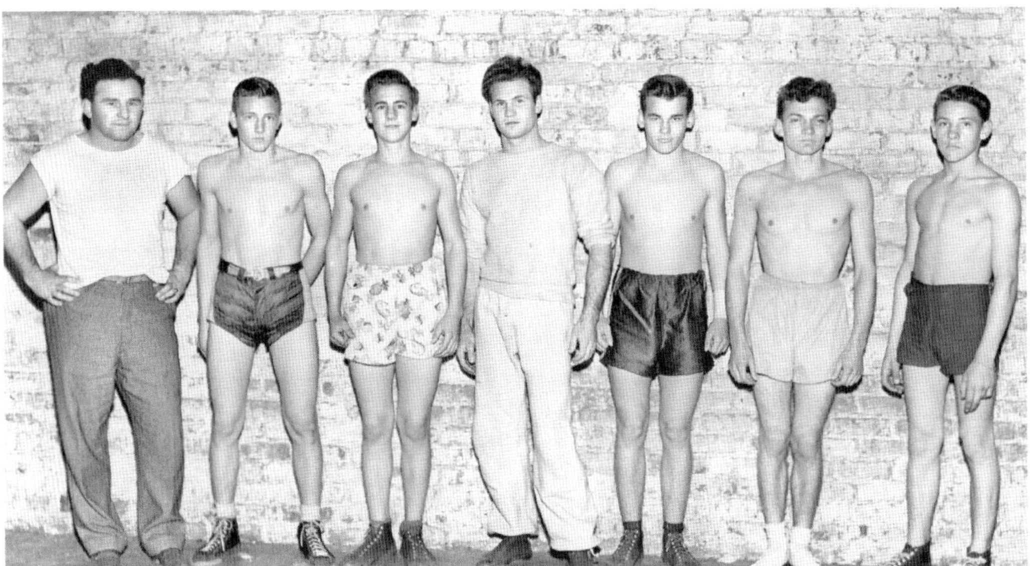

Coach Arnold Tarr and six Golden Gloves boxers from Lincolnton pose for this photograph for Charlotte's Golden Gloves Tournament, February 13–17, 1947. Coach Tarr was a former Golden Gloves champion in the middleweight division, and he predicted that he would "bring at least one and maybe two champions back to Lincolnton" after the tournament. From left to right are Coach Arnold Tarr, Steve Gabriel, Joe Fortenberry, Ray Little, Rathmul Helms, Carl Rudisill, and Jim Carter. (LCMH.)

Jack Dellinger stands ready to throw a few jabs and a right hook for this photograph from 1939. Dellinger trained with other boxers such as Ralph Connor and Bill Millburn at the old gymnasium in Lincolnton that was located in the basement of Lincolnton High School. At various points in their training, these men went to the Golden Gloves tournament in Charlotte that was held at the old Armory. Dellinger played football during the same time that he boxed (early 1940s) and played the clarinet in the band during his four years in high school. He left Lincoln County to fight in World War II in June 1943. He returned in 1945 and played one more year of high school football before graduating in 1946. He went to Catawba College for one year on a football scholarship. Upon completion of his freshman year, Dellinger went to work for First National Bank (1946–1948) and in 1953 went into the bottled gas business. He began selling insurance for New York Life in 1967, and continued in this business for over 30 years. (Courtesy of Jack Dellinger.).

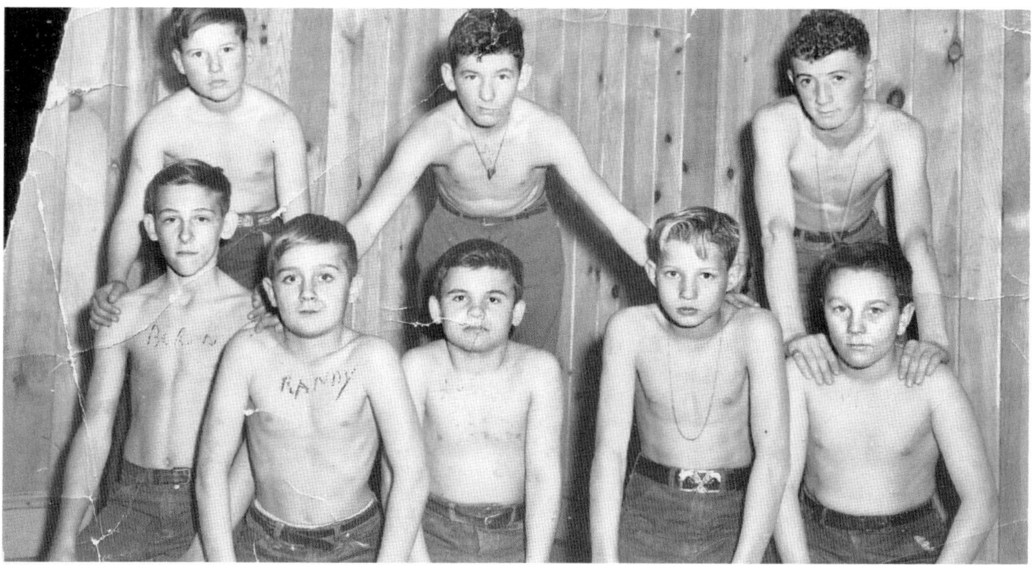

Aaron Lee Boyd stands over a group of young boxers at the old Lincolnton Recreation Center in 1952. From left to right are (first row) Johnny Burgin, Randy Ramsey, Buddy Setzer, John Bridges, and Billy Joe Goins; (second row) Bobby Keever, Aaron Lee Boyd, and Walter Reynolds. Boyd was an amateur flyweight during the 1950s and finished with 150 wins and 13 losses. In 1960, he earned a tryout for the Olympic Games. He was inducted into the Carolinas Boxing Hall of Fame in 2001 and the Lincoln County Sports Hall of Fame in 2004. (Courtesy of Lee Boyd.)

Ralph Connor provides a few tips to Jim Carter as the heavy bag waits for attention in the background. Connor has provided instruction to many athletes since the late 1940s. Jim Carter was a welterweight champion from Lincolnton. Over the years, Carter won Golden Gloves championships and "best boxer" awards in Gastonia, Hickory, High Point, and many other places. (Courtesy of Ralph Connor.)

Ralph Connor, physical education director of the Lincolnton VFW, accepts a trophy after a tournament with local boxers such as Lee Boyd and Sonny Taylor. (Courtesy of Ralph Connor.)

A charter member of Lincoln County Sports Hall of Fame, Roby Jetton (far right) held a 15-1 professional boxing record and lost only 19 out of 222 fights over the course of his career. He was inducted into the Carolinas Boxing Hall of Fame in 1999. (Courtesy of Roby Jetton.)

Ken "Chick" McCurry was a successful bantamweight and flyweight boxer during the early 1950s who trained under Angelo Dundee. He fought in 13 professional bouts and developed a youth boxing program at Lincolnton's VFW. Later called the Lincolnton Boxing Association, the program bred five national amateur champions and two professional fighters. McCurry coached for 30 years. His career culminated in his inclusion in the Carolinas Boxing Hall of Fame in 1990. He was inducted into the Lincoln County Sports Hall of Fame in 2005. (Courtesy of Ken McCurry.)

A prized trophy held by Jim Bost spawns ear-to-ear smiles from the Bear Ridge boxing team in 1965. Baby Ray Cornwell chose the Bear Ridge Pure Oil sign as a suitable backdrop for his photograph session. Team members are, from left to right, Junior Keener, Jerry McGill, Jim Bost, Johnnie Houser, Ronnie Houser, and Bruce Martin. (LCMH.)

As part of an illustrious boxing career, Billy Bridges received many medals and boasted a 22-2 professional record. He was ranked third nationally in the welterweight division in 1984–1985 and held an overall amateur record of 396-18. He held an international amateur record of 12-1; was Carolina Golden Glove Champion (1981–1986); Southern Golden Glove Champion, Knoxville, Tennessee (1982–1986); Southeastern Junior Olympic Champion (1977–1980); and Southeastern Open Regional Champion (1981–1986). He won the WBC Intercontinental Championship in the junior middleweight division and was ranked 12th in the world. (Courtesy of Ken McCurry.)

5

Betty G. Ross and the Lincolnton–Lincoln County Recreation Department

The name Betty Gabriel Ross is synonymous with sports in Lincoln County. Many young boys and girls swung their first tennis racket or swam their first laps in a pool that Ross helped build through her efforts as head of Lincolnton–Lincoln County Recreation Department. Ross lived in Boger City before assuming the position of director of the recreation department, organized by the City of Lincolnton, in 1947. A graduate of Appalachian State Teachers College's physical education program, Ross played basketball at Lincolnton High and participated in numerous sporting activities as a college student. Some of these activities include intramural manager of the woman's athletic association, president of the swimming club, team member of the women's varsity volleyball, basketball, softball, and speed ball teams, tennis and badminton doubles, and member of the Girls A Club. In addition, she directed a playground for a summer in Louisiana and, in 1946, served as the director of girls' activities at the YMCA in Fries, Virginia.

As Ross assumed the director's position in Lincolnton, the city planned to build a youth center that included a ballroom for dances and parties, a lobby for reading and playing cards, a snack bar, and an arts and crafts room. The youth center's basement housed bowling alleys, ping-pong tables, and a game room. The facility also included a playground with tennis courts, badminton area, and playground equipment. Under her supervision, the city sponsored a playground for Lincolnton's black community.

Over nearly 50 years, Betty G. Ross started tumbling classes, marble teams, and many other activities that served the youth of Lincoln County. To honor Ross's service, the local officials named a city park in her honor, and the Lincoln County Sports Hall of Fame inducted her in 2001.

The sign welcoming people into Betty G. Ross Recreation Park in Lincolnton stands as a testament to the long-lasting effect that Ross had on the physical education of young men and women over the course of 50 years. Dedicated in 1977, the park includes tennis courts, baseball and softball fields, a pool, and the William M. Lentz recreation building. (Courtesy of Betty G. Ross.)

Betty Ross wears her Lincolnton High sweater as she smiles with one of many groups with which she played. Along with Ross, Polly Miller (wearing street clothes) was the only player on the Green Creek team from Lincolnton. This was an All-Tourney Team that participated in a tournament in Valdese that was equivalent to a conference tournament. (Courtesy of Betty G. Ross.)

Tumbling was one of many programs that Betty Ross started after becoming director of the recreation department in 1947. Ross called this program Recreation Arts, and this group from the 1950s performed locally and out of town. Some team members include Frances Sisk, Beatrice Shidal, Jeannette Williams, Jan Rudisill, Pat Heavner, Barbara Moore, Janice Armstrong, Nancy Burgin, Frances Goins, and Diane Williams. (Courtesy of Betty G. Ross.)

A group of young gymnasts poses for a photograph by the Lincoln *Times-News* during the summer of 1977 at the recreation department's building on Pine Street. Led by local gymnastics instructor Jerry Gantt, these ladies took part in weekly practice; there was no other program in the area besides in Charlotte. Many of the young ladies became inspired to pursue gymnastics after Nadia Comaneci's gymnastics performance at the 1976 Olympics. (Courtesy of Betty G. Ross.)

A group of boys awaits a strike from Tommy Keever at the former recreation center on Pine Street during the early 1950s. Johnny Cromer is standing with the bowling ball in hand ready to follow Keever, and Neil Helms chats with the other boys on the side. (Courtesy of Betty G. Ross.)

Elizabeth Love bears a smile as she wears her Lincolnton Recreation Department T-shirt, ping-pong paddle, and award certificate. Love was the intermediate girls' ping-pong champion in 1952. (Courtesy of Betty G. Ross.)

Over the years, the recreation department had a winning marble tradition that took them to various state tournaments. Locally, the recreation department held their marble tournaments in the basement of the Old Crouse Elementary School. During the 1950s, the department took the local winner and runner-up to the state marble tournament in Greensboro. Darrell Harkey stands in the middle of the group of winners in the top photograph. (Courtesy of Betty G. Ross.)

The AMVETS Post 160 women's softball team in Lincolnton won runner-up honors in the Lincolnton recreation women's softball league during the summer of 1977. Team members are, from left to right: (first row) Truman Carter (manager), K. Sanford, K. Sigmon, F. Scronce, Nancy Parker, N. Blackburn, A. Holland, and J. Cherry; (second row) N. Hendricks, S. Smith, B. Beal, A. Propst, M. McCleave, K. Mayberry, D. Chapman, and L. Alexander. (Courtesy of Betty G. Ross.)

A ready and willing group of young athletes hangs on every word spoken by Coach John Mauney in 1969. The much-revered and well-remembered grandstand at Lincolnton High's Love Field stands tall in the background of this photograph. This edifice was a WPA project during the 1930s. John Mauney coached sports for the recreation department over the course of many years. (Courtesy of Betty G. Ross.)

Kids enjoy the recreation department's playground and swimming pool off North Cedar Street in Lincolnton during the late 1960s and 1970s. The recreation department, with Betty G. Ross as the director, first used the swimming pool in 1947 and welcomed many patrons before opening a pool at the local VFW and South Fork Recreation Park. The Chamberlain family, who owned a large home on North Cedar Street, built the wading pool. (Courtesy of Betty G. Ross.)

During the 1960s, the recreation department offered free tennis lessons with John Mauney to kids and teens in Lincolnton. A small group pauses for a moment for Betty Ross to capture their experience on the local tennis court at the corner of Congress and Academy Streets. Participants include Mike Ross, Joel Rudisill, Kathy Griggs, Butch Ross, Allen Reid, Pat Ross, Mary Ross, and Libby Ross. Below, some youngsters take part in the recreation department's free tennis lessons in 1970. (Courtesy of Betty G. Ross.)

A proud Grady Ray and Don Chapman (Vermont American Company uniform) hold trophies during the recreation department's presentation ceremony in 1971. Coaching legend Von Ray Harris (left) served as the department's athletic director each summer. (Courtesy of Betty G. Ross.)

Betty G. Ross presents a trophy to the boys of the High Shoals Recreation Midget Baseball championship team with Coach Howard Kiser looking on. The photograph was captured by Lincolnton photographer Don Frazier of Frazier's Studio. (Courtesy of Betty G. Ross.)

Betty Ross presents a winning trophy to a group from Long Shoals who were the lucky winners of an award from the Piedmont Area Development Association (PADA). (Courtesy of Betty G. Ross.)

A local photographer captures little-leaguer Mike Baker as he fields a ball on the diamond. During the time of this photograph, Baker played for the High Shoals Midget league. (Courtesy of Betty G. Ross.)

Standing on the recreation department's tennis courts in Lincolnton, doubles tennis champs Johnathan Rhyne and Tommy Andrews hold their trophies and rackets in 1974. (Courtesy of Betty G. Ross.)

A large group of kids surround Betty G. Ross during an Easter egg hunt sponsored by the recreation department in 1974. (Courtesy of Betty G. Ross.)

Coach Don Cagle stands with the recreation department's Junior Baseball League champs in 1975. Included in the photograph are, from left to right, Coach Don Cagle, Mike Caskey (MVP), Wes Beam (coach), and Buck Dellinger (coach). (Courtesy of Betty G. Ross.)

Long-time Lincolnton High Coach Von Ray Harris presents a trophy to Walt Heafner, Men's Softball MVP, in 1975. (Courtesy of Betty G. Ross.)

Coach Don Cagle stands with an unidentified MVP of Lincolnton's City league for this photograph that appeared in the Lincoln *Times-News* in 1976. (Courtesy of Betty G. Ross.)

The Lincoln County Hospital team, sponsored by Dr. Boyce Griggs, finished the 1977 playoffs as runner-up to Pumpkin Center in the Lincolnton Recreation Women's Softball League. The team defeated the AMVETS team, the regular season runner-up, to advance to the finals. From left to right are (first row) Judy Mann, Dr. Boyce Griggs (sponsor), Debbie Huffstetler, Kathy Scronce, and Mary Pound; (second row) Mike Allen (coach), Sherri Grigg, Teresa Allen, Paula Turner, Mary Brittain, Holly Lawing, and Bud Holt (manager); (third row) Nancy Davis, Peggy Simmons, Paula Odum, and Donna Littlejohn. (Courtesy of Betty G. Ross.)

A young girl takes a dive from atop the pool at the VFW swimming facility in Lincolnton in 1972. Below, a large group of local kids enjoy the water at the pool during a nice summer day. The recreation department taught swimming lessons at the VFW pool during the 1970s, prior to opening their own pool facilities at the Betty G. Ross Park in 1979. (Courtesy of Betty G. Ross.)

6

VFW Athletic Program

The VFW Shipp-Lockman Post 1706 Athletic Program began during the 1950s and sponsored many athletic programs that affected young men and women in sports such as marbles, boxing, baseball, basketball, and swimming. From marble tournaments at the old Crouse School basement in Crouse to bowling and boxing at the old recreation department building on Pine Street in Lincolnton, the VFW athletic program influenced many young men and women who utilized the lessons they learned to further their careers. The VFW sponsored many programs that extended beyond the athletic programs to include bloodmobiles, flagpoles to local schools, and Christmas parties for the underprivileged, but the most outstanding programs affected young athletes in the county.

The VFW athletic program, in conjunction with the local recreation department, trained many young men and women to become better student athletes. The program sponsored boxers, marble players, baseball players, softball, bowling, and high school sports awards. The marble program produced a number of local and state champions, and its sports program recognized local young men and women that stood out because of their sportsmanship and academic achievements. Ralph Connor served as the physical education director for many years and utilized his background in football, baseball, and boxing to instill in the young men and women of Lincolnton a winning spirit. Connor is responsible for helping build many local-, state-, and national-level marble winners and boxers such as Jim Carter, Lee Boyd, and Sonny Taylor. Ken "Chick" McCurry was another of the VFW's instructors; his boxing background contributed to his success with young men such as Billy Bridges, who held World Boxing Championship titles.

To honor Lincoln County veterans, the VFW built their current edifice in 1954 1955. The post awarded the contract to Seth Lumber Company in 1954 and planned construction at a cost of $48,389.50. The two-story building was constructed of cinder block, cement, and brick veneer. The ground floor included general and business offices, a meeting place, an athletic room with showers, and quarters for the caretaker. The second floor included a kitchen and banquet room with cloak rooms and restrooms, along with a dance floor. (Courtesy of Ralph Connor.)

One of the VFW's youth baseball teams occupies a set of bleachers for a photograph. The VFW's youth baseball program and other athletic programs received commendation from various county departments, such as the police and school administration, for their activities and contribution to elimination of juvenile delinquency. Each of these departments maintained a commitment to the VFW and its programs, cooperating in any way to ensure success. (Courtesy of Ralph Connor.)

Ralph Connor (far left), physical education director with the VFW, stands with a group of young men from Lincolnton that participated in one of many marble tournaments held at the old Crouse School. (Courtesy of Ralph Cannor.)

Darrell Harkey (right) and Gary Jenkins stand in the basement of the old Crouse School with their trophies after the 1956 Lincoln County Marble Championship. The recreation department and VFW cosponsored the event each year. Eleven-year-old Gary Jenkins was the county marble champion, and 14-year-old Darrell Harkey was runner-up. Jenkins was a student at Lincolnton Grammar School, and Harkey was a student at Love Memorial. (Courtesy of Ralph Connor.)

Each year, the VFW cosponsored marbles tournaments throughout Lincoln County. Organizers held tournaments for white kids at the old Crouse School, and the tournaments for black kids were held at Newbold High in Lincolnton. Many of the white kids that participated in the tournaments came from schools such as Lincolnton Grammar School, Love Memorial, Asbury, Iron Station, Hickory Grove, Crouse, Long Shoals, North Brook No. 3, and Triangle. The black marble players came from schools such as Mitchell, New Elbethel, Newbold, Oaklawn, Mount Vernon, and Rock Hill. Pictured at right is one of the marble tournament winners with a marble in hand and his prize-winning trophy to his right. Below is a group of young men who participated in a marble game or tournament off North Cedar Street in Lincolnton, at the park on the grounds of Park Elementary School. (Courtesy of Ralph Connor.)

Ralph Connor, above, far right, and another VFW member provide instruction to a few young boys who participated in a marble shoot at Park Elementary in Lincolnton during the early 1950s. A group of young men wait in the wings for an opportunity to work with the instructors. Though the young men participated in marble shooting at the below location, the basketball goal offered the young boys an opportunity to participate in another locally popular sport before or after their game. (Courtesy of Ralph Connor.)

Four young men stand with their championship trophies after the annual marble tournament sponsored by the VFW during the late 1950s in the Elizabeth City High gymnasium. The winners include, from left to right, David Lowery (11-year-old from Pembroke) with a sportsmanship trophy, Gary Jenkins of Lincolnton, a state champion who went on to the national tournament in Tallahassee, Florida; Steve Tsitouris, who finished third; and Philip Stamey of Valdese who finished as runner-up. In addition to their trophies, Jenkins and Stamey received bicycles. (Courtesy of Ralph Connor.)

Vicki Miller of Elkin and Gary Jenkins of Lincolnton hold their awards during a marble tournament in the Elizabeth City High gymnasium. Ralph Connor stands at the far right as a chaperone and physical education director for the Lincolnton VFW with other VFW officials from across North Carolina. Vicki Miller was crowned queen of the night by Virginia Lowery of Pembroke, who was president of the state VFW auxiliary. Gary Jenkins was the marble champion of North Carolina. (Courtesy of Ralph Connor.)

Two groups of marble players from Lincoln County and other North Carolina counties assemble for a photograph to document their participation in a large tournament. The girls wore sashes for their home cities, including Lincolnton, Albemarle, Elizabeth City, Greenville, Wilkesboro, Asheboro, Hendersonville, Hickory, Lincolnton, Durham, Plymouth, Elkin, and Farmville. (Courtesy of Ralph Connor.)

Ralph Connor, VFW physical education director, presents a trophy to an athlete from Lincolnton High during an award ceremony in the 1950s. (Courtesy of Ralph Connor.)

Ralph Connor presents Eli Reynolds an award from the VFW on April 28, 1952. Reynolds received the award as a member of the VFW's boys' basketball team. Betty Snipes also received a VFW award for her participation on the girls' basketball team. (Courtesy of Ralph Connor.)

Ralph Connor, second from right, Elizabeth Hoke, far right, and Coach Jack Kiser, second from left, stand with recipients during an award ceremony for Lincolnton High athletes sponsored by the VFW during the 1950s. Jack Kiser was one of the winningest coaches in Lincolnton High sports history, and Elizabeth Hoke was one of Lincolnton High's earliest women's coaches. (Courtesy of Ralph Connor.)

Ralph Connor and other officials from the VFW present trophies to three local young men who exhibited one of the criterion they used in their award determination. The committee gave awards to young men and women who participated in basketball, baseball, and football. These recipients did not have to be the most outstanding athletes but had to display sportsmanship on and off the field, scholastic attainment, all-around character and personality, and teamwork. Recipients had to be seniors with passing grades in all of their classes. (Courtesy of Ralph Connor.)

Ralph Connor, Jack Kiser, and other VFW officials presented awards to several female student athletes at a sports awards ceremony sponsored by the VFW during the 1950s. (Courtesy of Ralph Connor.)

Ken McCurry presents a boxing championship trophy to Jim King, manager of the VFW, around 1974. Ken was in charge of the boxing program. (Courtesy of Ken McCurry.)

The commander of the Lincolnton VFW presents a trophy in 1974 to a VFW-sponsored boxing group while they stand in the ring at the VFW. Some of the young boxers include Billy Bridges, Patrick Phelps, Frank Phelps, Rolando Galo, Steve White, Mark Ward, Trevor Ward, Jerome Hunter, Dennis Woods, Jeff Tyree, Calvin Cash, and Tim Johnson. (Courtesy of Ken McCurry.)

VFW boxer Alvin Fair holds up a strong left fist as he poses for the camera with his medal and trophy in 1991. Fair received this award for his performance at the Junior Olympic regionals. (Courtesy of Ken McCurry.)

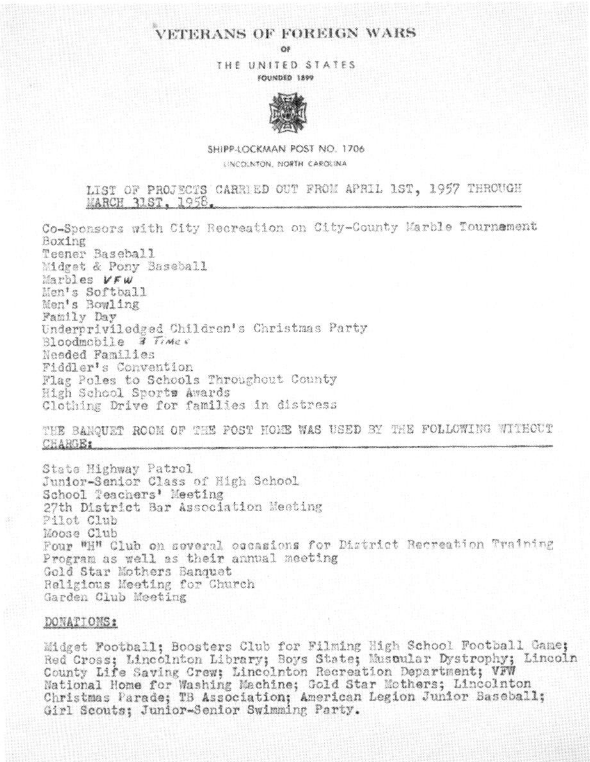

VETERANS OF FOREIGN WARS
OF
THE UNITED STATES
FOUNDED 1899

SHIPP-LOCKMAN POST NO. 1706
LINCOLNTON, NORTH CAROLINA

LIST OF PROJECTS CARRIED OUT FROM APRIL 1ST, 1957 THROUGH MARCH 31ST, 1958.

Co-Sponsors with City Recreation on City-County Marble Tournament
Boxing
Teener Baseball
Midget & Pony Baseball
Marbles VFW
Men's Softball
Men's Bowling
Family Day
Underpriviledged Children's Christmas Party
Bloodmobile 3 Times
Needed Families
Fiddler's Convention
Flag Poles to Schools Throughout County
High School Sports Awards
Clothing Drive for families in distress

THE BANQUET ROOM OF THE POST HOME WAS USED BY THE FOLLOWING WITHOUT CHARGE:

State Highway Patrol
Junior-Senior Class of High School
School Teachers' Meeting
27th District Bar Association Meeting
Pilot Club
Moose Club
Four "H" Club on several occasions for District Recreation Training Program as well as their annual meeting
Gold Star Mothers Banquet
Religious Meeting for Church
Garden Club Meeting

DONATIONS:

Midget Football; Boosters Club for Filming High School Football Game; Red Cross; Lincolnton Library; Boys State; Muscular Dystrophy; Lincoln County Life Saving Crew; Lincolnton Recreation Department; VFW National Home for Washing Machine; Gold Star Mothers; Lincolnton Christmas Parade; TB Association; American Legion Junior Baseball; Girl Scouts; Junior-Senior Swimming Party.

The VFW mailed out a list of projects from April 1, 1957, to March 31, 1958, to keep abreast of how many projects they accomplished. In addition to athletic activities, the post sponsored family days, Christmas parties, clothing drives, fiddlers' conventions, and flagpoles at schools throughout Lincoln County. Ralph Connor received various letters during his tenure from school administrators thanking the VFW for their support of Lincolnton High's sports. (Courtesy of Ralph Connor.)

Bryon Baker (left) hand Brandon Mitchem stand in the ring for a photograph in the Gastonia *Gazette* on Wednesday, April 6, 1988. North Carolina boasted seven Silver Gloves national champs, and three hailed from Lincoln County. Bryon Baker was an 80-pound, 11-year-old champ who won a Silver Gloves national title in his first year of competitive boxing, and Brandon Mitchem was the 75-pound, 10-year-old son of professional boxer Randy Mitchem. (Courtesy of Ken McCurry.)

7

Other Sporting Activities in Lincoln County

Lincoln County's athletic tradition expanded to include sports other than baseball, basketball, football, and boxing as the county built more elementary and middle schools and consolidated high schools in central Lincolnton and in the western and eastern parts of the county. Programs offered in Lincolnton through the recreation department and VFW and other programs in west and east Lincoln afforded young men and women an opportunity to participate in athletic activities such as tumbling, volleyball, soccer, wrestling, and golf. As Betty Ross introduced many of these activities and others such as ping-pong, Willie Hull brought basketball to many young men and women in the western part of the county.

Many residents contributed to athletics by offering their talents and support. Dr. Boyce Griggs sponsored local athletics by providing free physicals and treatments to athletes and sponsoring teams through monetary donations. Dr. Necip Ari, known as "the Boxing Doc," volunteered his time without any compensation as a ringside physician. Supporters such as Grady Abernathy, Kenny "Kojak" Hambright, and many others have contributed to the success of many teams throughout the county with their ever-present cheers, praise, and uplifting personalities.

A myriad of other sporting activities occupy the lives of many men and women in Lincoln County and are featured in the local newspaper and other media outlets. Lincoln County is fortunate to have bodybuilders, cyclists, and martial artists who are inspiring the county's new generation to exceed in activities outside of the traditional sports. There is no possible way to include all of these activities in a single volume of this size, but their hard work and excellence does not go unnoticed.

Jack Henry Ramseur (1911–1993) was well known for his kindness, wit, energy, saw playing, and wood carving abilities. He is photographed on the left in his gymnast uniform while at Davidson College, where he graduated in 1931. He was an avid volunteer, serving with Christian Ministry of Lincoln County and the American Red Cross. Ramseur was an elder at First Presbyterian Church and received the Governor's Award for Outstanding Service in 1990. He carved the Lincoln County Seal, which hangs in the county commissioner's chambers, out of Honduran mahogany. (LCMH.)

This group of women from the Boger and Crawford Mill village in Goodsonville (now Boger City) awaits a field day in the village. As the ladies pose in their softball uniforms from the late 1930s, the mill provides a background as a prominent landmark in the community. Robert Boger and his partner, Mr. Crawford, both of Philadelphia, built the mill in 1919, and by 1937, they employed 800 people. During the late 1930s, baseball and softball occupied the lives of many mill workers who lived and worked in the village. Each year, Boger hosted a field day and baseball game that featured athletic contests, games, boxing, and barbeque. Boger not only invited people who worked at the mill, but he also invited the general public. As advertised in the local paper, "everything is free but food and drinks." (Courtesy of David Napier.)

With cars and crowds surrounding an annual field day at Boger and Crawford Mills, the ladies of the mill's softball team occupy the diamond and help make the event a success for all involved. (Courtesy of David Napier.)

The West Lincoln High wrestling team has a long-standing record of winning in their conference and on the state level. In 2000, the Rebels wrestling team won their first state championship. The 2005 wrestling team wears their uniforms with pride for this yearbook photograph. (Courtesy of West Lincoln High School.)

Tearing up the turf on a sunny day on April 28, 2004, the North Lincoln girls' soccer team fought a hard battle against a worthy opponent from Polk County. The team that graced the field for North Lincoln includes players Jessica Bora (13), Kierstyn Cavazos, and Ashley Hooks. (Courtesy of Patty Skidmore.)

Dr. Boyce Griggs served Lincoln County citizens for over 42 years and as Lincolnton High's team physician for over 25 years. He established the Spark Plug award to honor athletes dedicated to their sport. He supported local efforts to build a new football stadium for Lincolnton High. He also made financial contributions to various women's softball teams. In addition, he attended many games as the sideline doctor. He was inducted into the Lincoln County Sports Hall of Fame in 2003. (Courtesy of Lincoln County Sports Hall of Fame.)

Completed in 1954, the "Block" Smith Gymnasium was built at a cost between $100,000 and $175,000 and includes three basketball courts. The gym accommodates 1,400 people and offers dressing rooms, locker rooms, showers, and toilet facilities for all athletes. A 40-foot-by-100-foot basement section was included as a correction facility to teach children how "to handle themselves." The building includes supply rooms, ticket rooms, first-aid rooms, a concession rooms, and public restrooms. The basketball court measures 100 feet by 100 feet and bears hardwood floors. (LCMH.)

Caldwell Nixon (1909–1995) was a born athlete. At 73, he jogged 10 miles a day. In 1982, he was a member of Gov. Jim Hunt's Council on Physical Fitness, an eight-person group that promoted physical fitness. He was a mortgage banker who was inspired to take on a fit life when he noticed how many of his colleagues were plagued with heart attacks and strokes. He was a member of the National Racquetball Association, the American Fitness and Running Association, the Denver Run Club, U.S. Men's Tennis Association, and the YMCA club in Charlotte. (LCMH.)

Dr. Necip Ari moved his OB-GYN practice to Lincolnton in 1975. Commonly know as the "Boxing Doc," he accompanied many boxers ringside before this position grew in popularity and necessity. The North Carolina Boxing Hall of Fame inducted him into their ranks in 1997, and he received the Dr. Ray Weason Physician of the Year award in 1987. He was present at over 30 national and 15 international boxing tournaments and at many of Billy Bridges's fights, and served as chief physician for the USA Boxing Association. He was inducted into the LCSHF in 2003. (Courtesy of Hilmi Ari.)

For 60 years, the Lincoln County Country Club has provided county citizens opportunities to indulge in golfing and swimming at one of the county's earliest recreational facilities. Kenneth Arrowood constructed the club's swimming pool, and Bruce Mashburn was in charge of the supervision and completion of the course. Mashburn was well known in North Carolina golfing circles for his work at Southern Pines, Pinehurst, Concord, Monroe, and Fort Bragg. His father was the greens keeper at Myers Park Country Club in Charlotte. (LCMH.)

With onlookers peering from the background, these four golfers pause for a photograph in 1947. The four men featured in the photograph were responsible for the opening of the Lincolnton golf course on July 2, 1947. Many spectators and golfers turned out for the function and participated in the success of the opening. From left to right are Mayor Dave Warlick, William "Buster" Lentz (secretary-treasurer), Dr. S. H. Steelman (vice president), and Joe Polhill (president). (LCMH.)

A photographer stops play to capture a few golfers at Lincoln County's new country club and golf course. Possibly participating in one of the club's many tournaments, these men would have registered for the event at the Lithia Inn bowling alley, located nearby. When the country club and golf course opened, James A. Abernathy Jr. allowed organizers to use this facility as the pro shop. Patrons indulged in the facility's swimming pool and used the club for private parties and entertainment, free of charge. (LCMH.)

Lincoln County golfers play nine holes at the Lincoln County Golf Course during the late 1940s. Completed in June 1947, the Lincoln County golf course has served many members of the county for 60 years. The total building costs for the land, golf course, swimming pool, and clubhouse were over $70,000. The country club has hosted various golf tournaments over in its history. (LCMH.)

Denver 100 was a cross-country motorcycle race that measured approximately 20 miles and ran through woods, fields, creeks, and even a barn. It was the main fundraiser for the Denver Volunteer Fire Department from 1974 through the late 1980s. Michael Lawing (73) traverses the Denver 100 course with other riders in the background in September 1988. (LCMH.)

A large group of people along the Denver 100 course jumped in to assist Michael Lawing (73) as he sought to distance himself from the competition. Dwight Callaway Jr. was the chief organizer of the race during its early days, with Worth Carswell taking over in the later years. In this photograph, Kirt Callaway stands in the middle of the muddy creek. At one time, the Denver 100 was the second largest and second longest-running motorcycle race in the nation. Organizers were fortunate to have as many as 403 riders in one year. In addition to the actual race, organizers produced patches, sun visors, T-shirts, tank tops, and other merchandise to raise money for the Denver Volunteer Fire Department. (LCMH.)

Todd Lawing stands at the directional arrow with the Denver 100 concession stand in the background in the late 1980s. Todd participated in the hare scramble, the motorcycle race for younger boys. In the photograph below, Todd (shirtless boy) stands with another racer and two other young race supporters in September 1988. (LCMH.)

The grass on which the young men of the hare scramble rode bears marks of many tires. Motorcycles of different sizes and from various companies stand in line with the help of the group before a race in Denver. (LCMH.)

The West Lincoln High cheerleading team boosts one of the members of the squad to show their team spirit and pump up the crowd during a basketball game. (Courtesy of West Lincoln High School.)

Micah Cline, Lincolnton High School softball player, stands ready to pitch a strike during the 1995 softball season. Cline began her softball career at an early age with the Boger City Boosters. She played at Lincolnton Middle School with Ann Anderson, where she found her niche as a pitcher. In high school, she again played for Coach Anderson and went on to be one of her team's leading hitters, winning the MVP and Gold Glove awards. During the summers, she played softball for a traveling team out of the West Lincoln area under Coach Randy Hull that traveled to Myrtle Beach, South Carolina, and Marion and North Wilkesboro, North Carolina. In 1995, with Micah as pitcher, the Lady Wolves finished second in the Western Piedmont AA conference and advanced to the state softball playoffs for the first time since 1990. Other members of the 1995 team included Leigh Goodson, Sherri Avery, Ashley Heavner, Misty Hallman, Amber Johnson, Marie Bumgarner, An Marcum, Kelley Helms, Abby Hill, Amy Pennell, Kylie Ballard, Amy Gates, Kristen Yoder, Jamie Boyles, Tara Dellinger, Jennifer Hoyle, Mindy Hovis, and Jamie Rhodes. (Courtesy of Micah Cline.)

Sources

Harpe, Jason. *Lincoln County*. Charleston, SC: Arcadia Publishing, 2000.

———. *Lincoln County Revisited.* Charleston, SC: Arcadia Publishing, 2003.

———. *Lincolnton: Photographs from the Clyde C. Cornwell Collection*. Charleston, SC: Arcadia Publishing, 2004.

Lincoln County Historical Association. *In Our Own Words: The Story of Lincoln County*. Norfolk, VA: Harris Connect, 2006.

Lincoln County News. Lincolnton, NC.

Lincoln County Sports Hall of Fame Induction Banquet Program. Lincolnton, NC: Lincoln County Sports Hall of Fame. 2001–2005.

Lincoln Times. Lincolnton, NC.

Sumner, Jim L. A *History of Sports in North Carolina*. Raleigh, NC: Division of Archives and History, NC Department of Cultural Resources, 1990.

INDEX